YOUNG STUDENTS
Learning
Library®

VOLUME 14

Merchant Marine — Mushroom

NEWFIELD
PUBLICATIONS

SHELTON, CONNECTICUT

CREDITS

Page 1668 Adrian Sington; 1669 ZEFA; 1678 British Museum; 1680 ZEFA; 1682 ZEFA; 1684 Trip/Richard Powers (top), Armando Curcio Editore (left center); 1685 ZEFA (top left), Scala (center right); 1686 Michigan Tourist Council; 1688 ZEFA; 1689 Picturepoint; 1693 Armando Curcio Editore; 1698 Frank Spooner; 1700 Bruce Coleman; 1702 Armando Curcio Editore (top), National Portrait Gallery (bottom); 1704 imitor; 1707 Kennecott Copper Corporation; 1710 Armando Curcio Editore; 1712 ZEFA (top), Minneapolis Convention & Visitors Commission (bottom); 1713 ZEFA; 1714 ZEFA; 1715 J. Allen Cash; 1717 Marconi; 1718, 1720 J. Allen Cash; 1721 ZEFA; 1722, 1723 ZEFA; 1725, 1726 ZEFA; 1727 Thorpe Park; 1728 Armando Curcio Editore; 1729 Armando Curcio Editore (top right), Dallas Museum of Arts (bottom left);

1730 Southern California Visitors Council; 1731 V. Kolpakov/ Trip; 1733 Heather Angel; 1736 Australian Company; 1738 ZEFA; 1739 National Gallery of Art, Washington D.C.; 1740, 1741 British Museum; 1742, 1744 ZEFA; 1745 Natural Science Photos; 1750 Montana Highway Commission; 1752 ZEFA; 1753 The Mansell Collection; 1754 ZEFA; 1758 NASA; 1759 Library of Congress; 1760 Photri (top), ZEFA (bottom); 1762 Mary Evans; 1764 Philip Grushkin (top left), Armando Curcio Editore (top right); 1760 ZEFA; 1769 Dom Morley; 1772 The Kobal collection; 1773 The Kobal Collection (top left), National Film Archive (bottom right); 1776 Rex Features; 1779 ZEFA; 1782 Armando Curcio Editore; 1786 Trip; 1789 ZEFA; 1790 ZEFA (top left), Natural History Museum (bottom left).

Young Students Learning Library and Newfield Publications are federally registered trademarks of Newfield Publications, Inc.

Copyright © 1994 by Newfield Publications, Inc.; 1974, 1972 by Funk & Wagnalls, Inc. & Newfield Publications, Inc.

Maps containing the appropriate Donnelley indication are copyright © 1994 by R.R. Donnelley and Sons Company. This product contains proprietary property of R.R. Donnelley & Sons Company.

Unauthorized use, including copying, of this product is expressly prohibited.

Printed in the U.S.A.

ISBN 0-8374-9821-X

CONTENTS

▲ A small village clings to the slope of a **MOUNTAIN** in the northern Andes, Venezuela.

MERCHANT MARINE

If you were going to take an ocean voyage, you would probably travel on a ship that belongs to some nation's merchant marine. Nonmilitary passenger and cargo ships make up a merchant marine. There are many fewer merchant-marine ships

Because the government recognizes the importance of having a strong merchant marine, it helps pay for the building and operation of some merchant ships. It also operates the U.S. Merchant Marine Academy at Kings Point, New York.

▼ Supertankers carry oil. These mammoth ships are more than 1,312 feet (400 m) long and carry up to 500,000 metric tons.

than there used to be because aircraft now carry most long-distance passengers and some freight too.

Many different kinds of ships are used by the merchant marine to transport different types of cargo. *Tankers* transport liquids, from delicate French wine to crude oil. *Container ships* carry goods already packed in large boxes or containers. *Freighters* usually carry dry cargo, such as grain. They sometimes carry a few paying passengers, too. Many people take holiday cruises on luxurious *ocean liners*. *Bulk carriers* transport heavy dry cargo, such as iron ore.

Merchant marine ships usually fly the flag of the countries where they are registered. The United States government regulates the U.S. merchant marine. The Coast Guard examines all merchant marine men and women for fitness and inspects ships to make sure they meet international safety standards. The U.S. Public Health Service checks to make sure health regulations are observed. The Maritime Administration of the U.S. Department of Commerce designs programs to aid the development and operation of the merchant marine. The Federal Maritime Board regulates merchant marine shipping.

▶ ▶ ▶ ▶ **FIND OUT MORE** ◀ ◀ ◀ ◀
Ships and Shipping;
Transportation

MERCURY

SEE SOLAR SYSTEM

MERMAID

In the harbor at Copenhagen, Denmark, perched on a rock, waves gently lapping around her, sits a statue of a mermaid. She has the body of a beautiful maiden down to her waist. Below that, she has the body and tail of a fish, glittering with shiny scales. She is a statue of the mermaid that Hans Christian Andersen wrote about in his popular fairy tale *The Little Mermaid*. Many songs, poems, and stories have been written about mermaids. And some legends tell of mermen as well as mermaids.

The mermaid is a creature from European legend. Mermaids are imaginary beings. They are supposed to live under the waters of oceans and rivers. The legends say that mermaids sometimes lure sailors

WHERE TO DISCOVER MORE

Andersen, Hans Christian. *Hans Andersen: His Classic Fairy Tales.* New York: Doubleday, 1978.

▲ Mermaids were said to sing enchanting songs that lured sailors to their doom.

▲ Hammurabi was king of Mesopotamia from about 1792 to 1750 B.C. He had the laws of the country gathered together into a code. It tells us much about life at the time of his reign.

WHERE TO DISCOVER MORE

Corbishley, Mike. *Ancient Rome.* New York: Facts on File, 1989.
Odijk, Pamela. *The Phoenicians.* New York: Silver Burdett Press, 1989.

to their deaths. They sit and comb their long golden hair and sing so sweetly that the bewitched sailors let their ships crash against the rocks. A rock in the Rhine River in Germany is the legendary haunt of a mermaid called the Lorelei.

The legends about mermaids may have been inspired by certain sea mammals called *dugongs* and *manatees.* These animals have long bodies, rounded heads, and fishlike tails. Sailors, seeing female manatees or dugongs off in the distance, nursing their babies, probably thought these mammals were mermaids.

▶▶▶▶ **FIND OUT MORE** ◀◀◀◀
Andersen, Hans Christian; Denmark; Manatee and Dugong

MESOPOTAMIA

The region of southwest Asia known as Mesopotamia is now part of the modern country of Iraq. Mesopotamia has a very ancient history. Several great civilizations of the ancient world flourished in the region, beginning about 5000 B.C.

Mesopotamia is a Greek name, meaning "between the rivers." The rivers are the Tigris and the Euphrates, both of which flow southeastward to the Persian Gulf. Mesopotamia is part of the so-called Fertile Crescent, which curves around from the Mediterranean Sea. Scientists believe that agriculture first developed in this area. Two groups of farmers and traders, the Sumerians and Akkadians, were living in Mesopotamia around 3000 B.C. They built one of the earliest civilizations in the world. The Sumerians invented an early form of writing known as *cuneiform.*

Mesopotamia became the center of the mighty Babylonian Empire after about 2000 B.C. Powerful invaders called Hittites overran Mesopotamia around 1550 B.C.

▲ By 3000 B.C., the Sumerians began using clay tokens in exchange for goods, instead of *bartering* (swapping for similar goods in value).

After the 1200s B.C., Mesopotamia was ruled by a succession of neighboring powers. These rulers included the Assyrians, the Persians, the Greeks, and the Romans. The Arabs drove the Romans out of the region in the A.D. 600s. The Ottoman Turks became rulers of Mesopotamia in the 1500s. They kept control until they were defeated

▲ A map showing ancient Mesopotamia. It lay between the Tigris and Euphrates rivers. At first the Sumerian cities ruled over the others, but about 2350 B.C., their power passed to the Akkadians.

in World War I (1914–1918). In 1921, Mesopotamia became a region of the independent nation of Iraq.

▶▶▶▶ **FIND OUT MORE** ◀◀◀◀
Agriculture; Ancient Civilizations; Babylonia; Greece, Ancient; Iraq; Ottoman Empire; Persia; Rome, Ancient

METABOLISM

All living things, both plant and animal, change food into living tissue and energy. The process by which this is done is called *metabolism.*

Metabolism begins with digestion. Food contains three main kinds of materials: *proteins, fats,* and *carbohydrates.* These materials are complicated chemical compounds that are broken down into simpler compounds during digestion. Metabolism eventually uses digested proteins (*amino acids*) to make muscle tissue. Most fats are stored in the cells of the body, and may be used to provide energy. Some carbohydrates are changed to fats and stored, while others are changed to a simple sugar, *glucose,* the main source of energy.

Amino acids and glucose pass through the walls of the intestine and into the bloodstream. Fats are collected by the *lymphatic system.* These food products are carried to all the cells of the body and stored or used.

Food materials cannot be used to provide energy without the process of *respiration.* Oxygen from the air passes through the lungs into the bloodstream. The blood takes oxygen to the cells, where it is used to burn sugar, often called "fuel." The burning produces energy. Some of this energy is heat that keeps the body at the proper temperature. The rest of the energy is used to move muscles, to send messages along nerves, and to build new tissues. These activities produce carbon diox-

ide and nitrogen-containing wastes. Carbon dioxide is carried to the lungs and exhaled. The nitrogen-containing wastes are carried to the kidneys by the blood and excreted.

Metabolism goes on more rapidly just after a meal and during exercise. If a person remains at rest for several hours after a meal, his or her metabolism settles down to its lowest rate. This rate is the person's *basal metabolism.* Rate of metabolism is an important sign of a person's health.

▲ **Each city-state had a temple tower (*ziggurat*). This is a reconstruction of the ziggurat at Ur, completed about 2100 B.C. On the top was the temple where the king, with the high priestess, performed religious rites and sacrifices.**

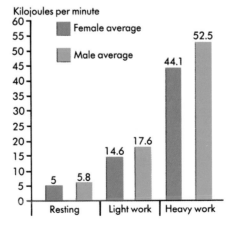

◀ **The rate at which the body uses energy varies depending on how hard we work. It is also different for males and females. When doing heavy work, we use up energy nine times as fast as when we are at rest.**

▶▶▶▶ **FIND OUT MORE** ◀◀◀◀
Carbohydrate; Digestion; Fats and Oils; Hormone; Human Body; Liver; Muscle; Nervous System; Photosynthesis; Protein; Respiration; Sugar

▲ Heat is *conducted* (carried) easily through metal objects. A metal spoon in a hot drink will get hot, while a plastic one remains cool.

▼ A collection of various metal objects commonly found around the home and office. The type of metal chosen to create an object, such as a nail or aluminum foil, depends on the metal's characteristics and the job the object will perform.

METAL

"See a pin and pick it up, and all the day you'll have good luck." A superstitious saying, but people living many years ago had a good reason to take care of their metal pins, nails, and needles. Since iron and steel were scarce and expensive, early American settlers straightened their bent nails so they could be used again, and took good care of their precious needles for sewing.

Metal plays a big part in our lives. Metals are taken out of the earth and processed to be used in small articles, such as nails, and in large articles, such as automobiles, buses, trains, and airplanes. Electricity is carried by wires made of metal. Large buildings are built on a metal framework. Water is brought into cities, and then into houses and other buildings through metal pipes. Although there are more than 80 metals, only about 20 are important in industrial use.

Characteristics of Metals

Metals vary, but a majority of metals share certain characteristics.

LUSTER. Most metals are *lustrous*, or shiny, when polished. Knives, forks, spoons, pans, and new pennies show the luster of metal. Some metals remain shiny for a very long time. Others soon get a dull surface because the metal combines chemically with the oxygen in the air. When metals become dull for this reason, we say that they are *tarnished* and need polishing. Iron combines very rapidly with oxygen when there is moisture in the air. The iron gets a covering of reddish brown scale called *rust*.

COLOR. Metals vary in color. Most are white, silvery white, or bluish white. Bismuth is pinkish white. Several are grayish white or steel gray. Cobalt is reddish gray. Copper is red, while gold and strontium are yellow.

MALLEABILITY. You can hammer or bend most metals into any shape you want. You can beat or roll them into thin sheets. Metals that can be easily shaped are called *malleable*. Gold is the most malleable metal. It can be hammered into sheets of gold leaf only 1/300,000 of an inch (1/100,000 of a centimeter) thick. Aluminum and silver are the two next most malleable metals.

On the other hand, a number of metals are brittle. They cannot be hammered, bent, or rolled without shattering. Among the brittle metals are bismuth, cobalt, and arsenic.

DUCTILITY. Some metals can be drawn out or stretched into wire. Such metals are *ductile*. Almost all the metals that are malleable are also ductile. Gold is the most ductile, and silver is second. Copper and aluminum also are ductile, and they are used for making wire, because they are more abundant and less expensive than gold and silver.

TENACITY. Most metals are *tenacious*, which means that they strongly resist being pulled apart. They are said to have *high tensile strength*. Tungsten (wolfram) and nickel are very tenacious, while lead, zinc, silver, and gold are not tenacious.

FUSIBILITY. Most metals are *fusible*—they can be melted fairly easily. One metal, mercury, melts at 38°F below zero (-39°C), and so it is found as a liquid at ordinary temperatures. Cesium and gallium will melt in the heat of your hand. Some metals have very high melting points and are not considered to be fusible. One of these is tungsten, which melts at 6,100°F (3,410°C).

CONDUCTIVITY. Most metals are good conductors of heat. This means that heat passes through them very well. The metals that conduct heat best are silver, copper, gold, and aluminum. Because aluminum conducts heat well and is cheap, many pots and pans are made of it. Poor conductors of heat are bismuth, mercury, and antimony.

Most metals are good conductors of electricity. Almost all metals are better conductors of electricity than are nonmetals. Silver is the best conductor of electricity. Aluminum and copper also are good conductors and are less expensive than silver.

HARDNESS. Metals vary quite a lot in hardness. Nickel, osmium, iron, and chromium are very hard metals. Lead, gold, potassium, and sodium are soft metals.

Metal Ores and Refining

All metals are taken from the Earth's crust. Aluminum makes up 8 percent of the Earth's crust, iron 4.5 percent, and calcium 3.5 percent. There is very little silver, gold, platinum, and iridium in the Earth's crust. That is

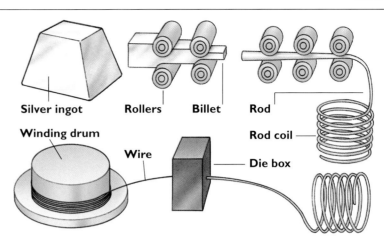

why they are rare and expensive. Metals found in the ground with surrounding materials are called *ores*.

A small number of metals are found pure in the earth. Gold, silver, and some copper are three of these metals. This fact explains why gold, silver, and copper were used by people in prehistoric times.

Most metal ores consist of a metallic element combined with elements that are not metals. Oxygen is the main nonmetal with which ores combine. Iron ore is made up of iron and oxygen; iron, carbon, and oxygen; or iron and sulfur. Tungsten ore consists of tungsten, iron, and oxygen. *Metallurgy* is the science of extracting or taking metals from their ores and *refining* them for use in manufacturing. There are several ways of refining ores. The one most used is *smelting*, in which the ore is melted, generally with carbon. In smelting iron, heat causes carbon to combine with the oxygen of iron ore, leaving pure iron. This process was discovered at least 4,000 years ago.

To remove sulfur from metal ore, the ore is *roasted* in air. The oxygen of the air combines with the sulfur, forming a gas and leaving pure metal. This is how the iron-sulfur ore is refined.

Leaching is another way to get metal from ore. A chemical is used to dissolve the metal out of the ore. In a second step, the metal is removed from the chemical in which it is dissolved. Leaching is used to remove gold from certain gold ores.

▲ **Many metals, including aluminum, gold, iron, copper, and silver, are ductile. This means they can be drawn into wire and hammered or rolled into various shapes without breaking.**

IMPORTANT MINERALS

Bauxite (aluminum ore): main producers: Australia, Jamaica, Guinea

Copper: main producers: Chile, the United States

Gold: main producers: South Africa, Canada, Russia, the United States

Iron ore: main producers: Brazil, Australia, China

Lead: main producers: the United States, Australia, China

Silver: mined in more than 54 countries

Tin: main producers: Malaysia, Bolivia, Indonesia

Uranium: main producers: the United States, Canada, South Africa

Zinc: main producers: Canada and many other countries

LEARN BY DOING

Metal *fatigue* is the weakening of metal caused by the repeated pushing, pulling, and rubbing of metal in the normal use of a machine. Find some steel or copper wire or ask for an old aluminum alloy teaspoon. Bend the wire or spoon back and forth many times.

Eventually the metal will weaken so much that it will split or snap in half.

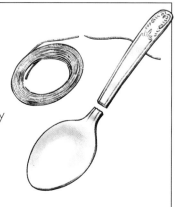

▲ Bronze was the first man-made alloy. It was often used to make armor and weapons.

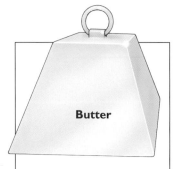

Butter

Gold Lead Tin Aluminum

Metals have a very high *density* (weight per volume). Just a small piece of gold weighs the same as a large lump of butter.

Still another way of getting metal from ore is to use an electric current, by *electrolysis*. The current is run through a solution of the ore. The atoms of the metal, which have a positive electric charge, move through the solution and collect on a negatively charged metal plate hung in the solution. This is how aluminum is separated from its ore.

Alloys

Most metals are not used in their pure state. The usefulness of metals can be very much improved by combining them. This is done by melting the metals and dissolving one in another. The result is an *alloy*. From two to seven metals may go into the making of an alloy. People learned to make alloys at least 6,000 years ago, when they learned to make bronze. Bronze is an alloy of copper and tin. For more than a thousand years, people made arrowheads, axes, swords, cooking pots, fishhooks, ornaments, and many other things from bronze. Bronze is still used for statues and ship fittings. Brass, an alloy of copper and zinc, is another common copper alloy. Most coins are made of cupro-nickel, an alloy of copper and nickel.

The most important modern alloys are those of iron, aluminum, magnesium, and titanium. Steel is an alloy of iron and carbon (which is a nonmetal) with some other metals. The most important alloys of aluminum are Duralumin (aluminum with copper, magnesium, and manganese) and

magnalium (aluminum and a small amount of magnesium). Both of these alloys are used in the making of automobiles.

To make useful objects, a metal such as iron is *forged* or changed from a bar into shapes by heating. A blacksmith makes a horseshoe by heating iron and hammering it into shape. Iron can be twisted and bent into shapes, such as *wrought iron* railings, or it may be *cast* (melted and poured into molds).

Micrometallography has helped scientists study what metals are made of and how they change when treated. This process is the photographing of a small section of a metal, magnified by a microscope.

▶ ▶ ▶ ▶ **FIND OUT MORE** ◀ ◀ ◀ ◀
Earth; Earth History;
Mineral

METAMORPHOSIS

Did you know that a caterpillar turns into a butterfly? That a tadpole becomes a frog or toad? Many insects and amphibians go through a series of changes during growth, called *metamorphosis*. As the young animal grows into an adult, its whole body form changes. The adult body form is usually very different from the younger body form.

Insect Metamorphosis

Insect metamorphosis has four stages *egg*, *larva*, *pupa*, and *adult*. Insects that must go through all four stages are said to go through *complete metamorphosis*.

LARVA. The larva is the insect form that hatches from the egg. The outer skin of the larva dries and hardens within a few hours after hatching. This skin, or cuticle, is made of a tough material called *chitin* that protects the larva's soft body. The larva crawls around in search of food. Its mouth is made for feeding on leaves or grasses. As the larva grows, it sheds its skin three to nine times. This is called *molting*. The hard chitin cannot grow or stretch with the body of the larva. The larva must shed the old skin that has become too small and grow a new skin that will fit.

If you watch a fly egg hatch, you will see the fly larva, a wormlike *maggot*, appear. The larva of a moth or butterfly is called a *caterpillar*. You can see that these larvae are very different from their adult forms.

PUPA. When the larva has grown to a certain size, it is ready for the pupa stage. At this time, the insect stops moving about and looking for food. Some larvae, such as caterpillars, spin cocoons around themselves. Others, such as cutworms, burrow into the ground. During the pupa stage, the insect does not move or eat. It spends the whole time changing into its adult form. The wings, legs, eyes, antennae, and other parts of the adult body develop.

Silkworms spin cocoons from threads of sticky fluid made by special glands. People can steam and unwind these silk threads and weave them into fine silk cloth.

ADULT. The adult form of an insect is called an *imago*. When the pupa is fully developed, it breaks out of its cocoon or its underground burrow. At first, the insect's wings are crumpled and soft. Body fluids are pumped into the wings to make them unfold. The insect exercises its new wings until they become dry and stiff. Then it is able to fly away.

INCOMPLETE METAMORPHOSIS. Wingless insects and other types, such as grasshoppers, locusts, and dragonflies, do not go through all three stages of complete metamorphosis. They go through *incomplete metamorphosis*. The larva of an insect that goes through incomplete metamorphosis is called a *nymph*. Nymphs are very similar to the adult

▲ Every butterfly goes through four different stages in its life cycle. 1. It starts as an egg. 2. It hatches into a caterpillar (larva). 3. Next, it turns into a pupa. 4. Finally, it becomes an adult.

forms, but they are smaller and their wings and other body parts are not fully developed. The nymph gradually changes into an adult by growing and molting. The nymph looks more like an adult each time it sheds its skin. When it molts for the last time, the adult insect appears.

Some cicadas have an unusual metamorphosis. After the nymphs hatch, they live underground for 17 years. They eat roots and grow, molting every so often. They tunnel out of the ground in the spring of the seventeenth year when they are ready for their last molt. They attach themselves to a surface, molt for the last time, and fly away.

Amphibian Metamorphosis

Frogs and toads also go through a metamorphosis. Eggs are laid in the water, and they hatch into larvae, called *tadpoles*. A tadpole has a round body with a tail, and breathes through gills like a fish. As it gets older, the gills and tail disappear, and

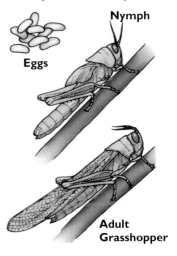

Incomplete metamorphosis

Nymph

Eggs

Adult Grasshopper

▲ Grasshoppers go through a *nymph* stage of developing and molting several times before they reach adulthood.

1675

Scientists have discovered that the metamorphosis of frogs is caused by a substance called "thyroxin" that is produced by the thyroid gland. If the thyroid gland of a tadpole is removed, the tadpole will continue to grow, but it will never turn into a frog. It becomes a monster tadpole.

lungs develop. A pair of hind legs grows and then a pair of front legs. Finally, the adult frog or toad comes out of the water and can live on land. Amphibians change gradually from larva to adult.

▶▶▶▶ **FIND OUT MORE** ◀◀◀◀
Amphibian; Bee; Butterflies and Moths; Egg; Fly; Frogs and Toads; Growth; Insect; Mosquito; Silk

METEOR

The "shooting star" that streaks across the sky is a tiny particle or piece of matter from outer space. When the particle enters the Earth's atmosphere, friction with the air causes it to glow white hot and then to turn to gas. Most of these particles, or *meteors*, are smaller than a grain of rice.

On a dark night, you can count six or seven meteors an hour. On special nights, though, you may see a *meteor shower*. Then you can count 60 or more meteors an hour! The second week in August is a good time to see a meteor shower.

Many meteors seem to be fragments of comets that crashed into one another. Other meteors are tiny particles from the tails of comets. Some meteors are iron and others are stone.

Once in a while, an extra bright meteor, or *fireball*, appears. Fireballs can sometimes be seen during the day and may even be as bright as the full moon. Some meteors survive their fall through the Earth's atmosphere

▲ A meteor, or shooting star, is caused when an object enters the Earth's atmosphere and burns up.

▼ About 25,000 years ago an iron-nickel meteorite, up to 260 feet (79 m) across, gouged a 575-foot (175-m) deep hole in Arizona. Known as the Coon Butte Crater, it is one of the world's largest meteorite craters.

and land on the ground. These are called *meteorites*, and—surprisingly—they are usually cool enough to touch when they land.

Most meteorites are small. But big meteorites hit the Earth sometimes. These huge meteors explode when they hit the ground and dig out craters. The largest proven crater is in Arizona. It is about 4,150 feet (1,265 m) across and 575 feet (175 m) deep. Its sides are 130 to 155 feet (40 to 48 m) higher than the ground around the hole. The moon and the planets Mercury and Mars are covered by such craters because they have no air to burn up meteors that strike them and no weather to erode the craters.

▶▶▶▶ **FIND OUT MORE** ◀◀◀◀
Astronomy; Comets

METEOROLOGY

SEE WEATHER

METRIC SYSTEM

A system of units of measure devised by the French Academy of Sciences has been used in France since the French Revolution. It has the great advantage of being a *decimal system* (based on a factor of 10). This means that you do not have to remember a large number of factors, such as the number of inches in a foot (12) or the number of pints in a gallon (8). In metric units, the factor is always 10.

In Europe, the metric system has been in use for most of this century. Other countries around the world, such as Canada and Great Britain, have adopted the metric system, too. The U.S. government passed a law in 1975 establishing conversion to the metric system by 1990. However, this has not yet happened, and many Americans are opposed to conversion.

In 1960, scientists throughout the

world adopted a form of the metric system, called the International System of Units, for use in science. Some of the main SI units (the agreed abbreviation for the French *Systeme Internationale*) are the meter, kilogram, second, and ampere. Using these units, scientists and engineers from all countries are able to understand each other without confusion.

▶ ▶ ▶ ▶ **FIND OUT MORE** ◀ ◀ ◀ ◀
Measurement

Metric Prefixes	Symbol	Multiplication	Power of 10
tera-	(T)	x 10,000,000,000,000	= 10^{12}
giga-	(G)	x 1,000,000,000	= 10^9
mega-	(M)	x 1,000,000	= 10^6
kilo-	(k)	x 1000	= 10^3
hecto-	(h)	x 100	= 10^2
deca-	(da)	x 10	= 10^1
deci-	(d)	x 0.1	= 10^{-1}
centi-	(c)	x 0.01	= 10^{-2}
milli-	(m)	x 0.001	= 10^{-3}
micro-	(μ)	x 0.000001	= 10^{-6}
nano-	(n)	x 0.000000001	= 10^{-9}
pico-	(p)	x 0.00000000001	= 10^{-12}

MEXICAN AMERICANS

Mexican Americans are an important and growing minority in the United States. Nearly 13.5 million U.S. citizens described themselves as Mexican Americans in the 1990 Census. They make up the largest group of Hispanic Americans. Only black Americans form a larger minority in the United States. About four out of five Mexican Americans live in the major cities of the west and southwest.

The number of Mexican Americans is growing rapidly. The 1990 Census total showed an increase of nearly 5 million Mexican Americans. That increase alone was more than half of the 1980 Census total! About 1.6 million of these people were new immigrants from Mexico.

Most Mexican Americans are *mestizos*, descendants of the native tribes and Spanish colonists of Mexico. The Spanish also penetrated the southwest region of what is now the United States in the 1500s.

Mexican Americans face many difficulties in their new country. Language and education are the main obstacles they confront in their attempts to improve their condition. Most speak Spanish and grow up with little or no command of the English language.

Education is a serious problem. This is partly because many Mexican American families are migrant work-

ers—they move from place to place. Children attend school irregularly.

Mexican Americans have the poorest record for completing a high school education. In 1970, only a very few Mexican American adults had completed high school. By 1991, the figures showed an improvement, nearly one in two completed their schooling, but that was still worse than any other group.

The problems with language and education mean that too many Mexican Americans are forced to take low-paying jobs. Then, with a large family trying to live on a low income, children are expected to help support the family. That means the poor education of one generation leads to the poor education of the next.

▲ The metric system, so-called because it began with the meter, or *metre*, is a decimal system of units. Multiplying or dividing numbers is easy, because it only involves changing the position of the decimal point.

▼ Mexican Americans enjoy the benefits of a dual culture—Mexican traditions in the United States. This family is about to eat a traditional Mexican meal.

Background of the People

Mexican Americans have a long and proud history, both in Mexico and in the United States. It is also a troubled history, with conflict as well as cooperation defining their relationship with Spain and later the U.S.

Several advanced Indian civilizations developed in Mexico as early as 3,000 years ago. The Olmecs and Mayas on the Gulf coast, and later the Toltecs and Aztecs in the central highlands, built towering pyramids and large irrigation systems.

The reign of the Indians came to an end in 1521, when Hernando Cortés and his 600 *conquistadors* (conquerors) claimed Mexico for Spain. Spanish rule continued for 300 years. Most Mexicans adopted the Spanish language and the Roman Catholic faith. There was also intermarriage between the Indians and Spanish. Before long, most Mexicans were people of mixed Indian and Spanish ancestry (mestizos).

Spanish Mexico included much of what is now the West and Southwest of the United States. The people who founded cities such as Los Angeles, Albuquerque, and Tucson were the first Mexican Americans. Santa Fe, New Mexico, was founded in 1609, 11 years before the Pilgrims landed at Plymouth, Massachusetts.

Mexico became independent in 1821. The new nation included all of what are now the states of Arizona, California, Colorado, Nevada, New Mexico, Utah, Wyoming, and Texas.

Under the Stars and Stripes

Two events in the 1800s turned thousands of Mexicans into Mexican Americans overnight. U.S. settlers in Texas declared independence from Mexico in 1836. Twelve years later the United States gained the rest of the region after defeating Mexico in the Mexican War. Mexicans living in this part of North America at this time automatically became American citizens.

At first the Mexican Americans and the white American settlers lived together peacefully. White settlers learned how to irrigate and grow crops on the dry land. They also learned Mexican techniques for prospecting for gold and for rounding up cattle. The Mexicans' Spanish terms for many things crept into the language. New words included "ranch," "lasso," and "canyon."

Life in the Barrio

Tensions soon arose between the two groups. Most white Americans did not mix with the Mexican Americans because of differences in language and religion.

Many Mexican American families lost their claims to land because they could not understand the English language on the legal forms. They, and the thousands of Mexicans who continued to immigrate to the United States, were forced to move to the cities to find work.

Mexican Americans remained separate from their white neighbors even when they moved to the cities. Racial prejudice and the language differences meant that most Mexican Americans had little choice but to live in the worst housing. They had separate churches, stores, and schools. These *barrios* (neighborhoods) were almost always in the poorest districts of the cities.

Mexican American community leaders set up organizations to improve conditions in the early 1900s. The League of Latin American Citizens, founded in 1929, set out to improve working conditions by forging links with labor unions. The Mexican American Political Association, founded after World War II, aimed to fight discrimination.

▲ The Mayas built this pyramid at Chichén Itzá on the Yucatán Peninsula, Mexico, more than 1,000 years ago. It was used for religious ceremonies.

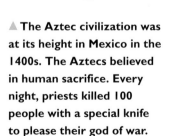

▲ The Aztec civilization was at its height in Mexico in the 1400s. The Aztecs believed in human sacrifice. Every night, priests killed 100 people with a special knife to please their god of war.

Renewed Pride

Black Americans' struggle for civil rights in the 1950s and 1960s awakened a sense of pride and injustice among many Mexican Americans. They took the term *Chicano*, which was once an insult, and turned it into a proud source of identity. They also became politically active. In fact, since the 1970s, Mexican Americans have been elected or appointed to many high-ranking political positions.

Community workers in the barrios continue to encourage Mexican Americans to register to vote, so that their increased political involvement will help to improve conditions. School systems in cities such as Chicago and Los Angeles are now responding to calls for more Spanish-speaking teachers.

Mexican Americans have already achieved success in many areas. Sports stars such as Lee Trevino and Fernando Valenzuela have become heroes to all Americans. The writers Rodolfo Acuna, Ernesto Calarza, Tomas Rivera, and Luis Valdez portray the vibrant past and present of Mexican-American life. Musicians such as Los Lobos have achieved international fame with their songs about barrio life.

▶▶▶▶ **FIND OUT MORE** ◀◀◀◀

Aztecs; Conquistadors; Cortés, Hernando; Hispanic Americans; Mayas; Mexico; Mexican War; Spanish-American War; Spanish History

MEXICAN WAR

The Mexican War between the United States and Mexico lasted from 1846 to 1848. It started when the United States was trying to gain more territory in the West. This territory belonged to Mexico and included what are now Texas, New Mexico, Arizona, Utah, Nevada, California, and parts of Wyoming and Colorado.

During the early 1800s, many U.S. settlers had moved into Mexico's land (especially into Texas) because it was unoccupied and undefended. In 1836, Texas settlers defeated Mexican troops and made Texas an independent republic. Texas was granted statehood in 1845. The United States claimed that the Rio Grande was the southern boundary of Texas. The Mexicans said the boundary was at the Nueces River. Mexico and the United States both claimed the land between the two rivers.

President James Polk wanted U.S. territory to extend all the way to the Pacific Ocean. When peaceful negotiations failed between the U.S. and Mexico, Polk ordered General Zachary Taylor to move some troops to Corpus Christi, Texas. Corpus Christi was on the land that both

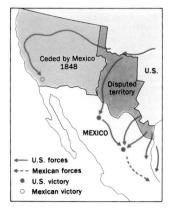

▲ On April 25, 1846, American soldiers moved into the disputed territory. The Mexican army retaliated by entering the area also, and the U.S. declared war.

◀ Scott's forces landed at Veracruz and won victories against the Mexicans at Cerro Gordo and Churubusco before taking Chapultepec (seen below). They went on to capture Mexico City on September 14, 1847. Five months later, the Treaty of Guadalupe Hidalgo was signed.

The daring divers of La Quebrada cliffs, Acapulco, are a local attraction for tourists. Diving 120 feet (37m) into a shallow cove, the divers have to time the highest waves accurately, so that they dive into deep enough water.

Mexico and the U.S. claimed to own. The Mexican government claimed that General Taylor had invaded Mexico. A Mexican army, led by General Mariano Arista, attacked Taylor's troops. War had begun.

Antonio López de Santa Anna was a former president of Mexico who wanted to get back into power. He agreed to sign a treaty giving the United States the Mexican land it wanted if Polk would help him get back into power. Santa Anna regained the presidency in 1846, but he refused to give up any Mexican lands.

Polk ordered General Winfield Scott to attack Mexico City. Santa Anna attacked Taylor's troops but was beaten. On September 14, 1847, Scott's forces captured Mexico City.

On February 2, 1848, the Treaty of Guadalupe Hidalgo was signed. This peace agreement gave the United States the territories of California, Arizona, Nevada, Utah, and part of New Mexico. It also set the border of Texas at the Rio Grande. In return, Mexico received $15 million. Shortly after peace was signed, gold was discovered in California, the gold rush began, and with it a new period of expansion.

▶ ▶ ▶ ▶ **FIND OUT MORE** ◀ ◀ ◀ ◀

American History; Mexican Americans; Mexico; Polk, J. K.; Rio Grande; Taylor, Zachary; Texas

▼ Acapulco lies on a beautiful bay, 190 miles (300 km) southwest of Mexico City, below the range of Sierra Madre del Sur.

 # MEXICO

The United States of Mexico is the southern neighbor of the United States of America. Mexico is about three times the size of Texas. It is the land of the ancient Maya and Aztec Indians. In Mexico today, you can see modern cities, volcanoes, snow-capped mountains, and beautiful beaches. The country is divided into 31 states and a federal district. The capital, Mexico City, is located in the Federal District, as Washington is in the District of Columbia.

Land

Mexico has the Pacific Ocean to the west. On the east are the Gulf of Mexico, the Caribbean Sea, and parts of the Atlantic Ocean. On the north, its border with the United States is about 1,600 miles (2,500 km) long. The Rio Grande flows along part of it. The small nations of Guatemala and Belize lie to the south of Mexico.

Mountains cover two-thirds of the country. Twenty-two Mexican mountain peaks are more than two miles high. The highest is Citlaltépetl (Orizaba) 18,701 feet (5,700 m) high. Many are volcanoes, including the famous Popocatépetl and Ixtaci-huatl, both more than 17,000 feet (5,000 m) high. Popocatépetl means "the hill that smokes" and Ixtaciu-atl means "the sleeping lady" in the Aztec language. Earthquakes sometimes shake the ground. One severely damaged Mexico City in 1985.

The Sierra Madre Occidental mountains run down the west side of Mexico, and the Sierra Madre Oriental run down the east side. The land between is high and flat. Most Mexicans live on this central plateau, and nearly all large Mexican cities are at least 5,000 feet (1,500 m) above sea level. Three exceptions are Monterrey, a major industrial city near the Texas border, and the two seaports on the Gulf of Mexico, Veracruz and Tampico.

Narrow, sandy coastal plains separate the mountains from the sea. Baja California, a narrow mountainous peninsula, extends southward from the state of California. The Yucatán peninsula is a low, level region on the Gulf of Mexico. The Maya Indian civilization was here.

On the central plateau, Guadalajara, Mexico's second largest city, is noted for its mining and agriculture and its pottery and glassware. The city of Cuernavaca, which means "the horn of a cow," has a splendid palace built by Cortés, the Spanish conqueror of Mexico. Murals by the modern Mexican painter, Diego Rivera, now decorate the palace. Taxco, a high mountain town known for its silver, is located south of Mexico City.

Climate
South and southeastern Mexico and the seacoasts have a hot, humid climate. The beach resorts of Acapulco and Puerto Vallarta are on the Pacific coast. In the north, much of the land is desert—scorching hot and dry in summer, sometimes freezing cold in winter. The climate of the central part of the country is not so harsh. The altitude keeps the weather mild and temperate. Most of the rain falls in the summer. The year-round average temperature is from 60° to 65° F (15° to 18°C).

Natural Resources
Mexico has many valuable mineral deposits. Copper is mined in the northwest; coal in the northeast; iron ore and sulfur in the southwest; and gold, silver, lead, and zinc in the central region. Much oil is found on the east coast, beneath the waters of the Gulf of Mexico.

One-sixth of Mexico is forest country, where lumbering is an important industry. Mahogany comes from the tropical forests. Fig trees and coconut palms grow along the coasts. Oak, ash, walnut, poplar, and gum trees grow in the plateau forests, while pines, cedars, and firs grow on the mountainsides.

Many fish and shellfish are caught in Mexico's coastal waters. Shrimp,

MEXICO

Capital city
Mexico City
(18,748,000 people)

Area
761,605 square miles
(1,972,547 sq. km)

Population
85,784,000 people

Government
Federal republic

Natural resources
Oil, silver, gold, uranium, coal, lead, zinc

Export products
Petroleum and petroleum products, cars and trucks, fertilizers, minerals

Unit of money
Peso

Official language
Spanish

The Spanish explorer Cortés was once asked by someone in Spain what Mexico looked like. Cortés crushed some parchment in his hand and threw it on the table. "There," he said, "that is the map of Mexico!" The explorer was trying to explain that Mexico is a land of soaring mountains, tropical jungle, burning deserts, and swamps.

© 1994 GeoSystems, an R.R. Donnelley & Sons Company

▲ The Olmecs were Stone Age inhabitants of Mexico. They carved huge heads, some of them more than 9 feet (3m) tall.

▲ A sculpture from Teotihuacán, a powerful city-state in the highlands of Mexico during the 400s.

▶ The Toltecs were a warring race of people, who lived in central Mexico from the 900s to the 1100s. They worshipped the god Quetzacoatl, whose temples were guarded by stone statues of warriors.

oysters, abalones, red snappers, sardines, and swordfish are popular.

Corn is the most important grain grown in Mexico. Other grain crops are wheat, rice, and barley. Sugarcane, coffee, tobacco, and bananas also are grown. Mexico is one of the world's largest suppliers of sisal, used for making rope. Cattle, pigs, poultry, and sheep are Mexico's main livestock.

Factories in Mexico produce textiles and paper, as well as leather goods, cement, pottery, and glass. Food and tobacco are processed, and sugar is refined.

One of the most important industries in Mexico is tourism. While sightseeing, visitors to the country will notice the temples and pyramids of ancient native civilizations, as well as modern apartments, hotels, and office buildings.

People
One-half of all Mexicans live in big towns and cities, while the other half live in villages, farms, and ranches. In the cities, many people live and work in modern buildings and carry on a busy industry. About one-third of the Mexican people still live as the poorer natives did before the Spanish conquest. Their diet is largely corn, chili, and beans. They wear *huaraches* (sandals) or go barefoot, and sleep on *petates* (straw mats) on the floor. Most Mexicans today are of mixed Spanish and Indian descent. The people speak Spanish and most are members of the Roman Catholic church.

▲ Many Mexicans are Roman Catholics, and they celebrate their religious festivals with processions and parties.

History
In the area called Oaxaca, long before the birth of Christ, early native people constructed magnificent palaces, temples, and pyramids. They studied the stars and developed fine arts such as sculpture, painting, weaving, and pottery.

By the time the Spanish arrived from Europe in 1519, other native people, called the Aztecs, had built a large capital, called Tenochtitlán, on the site where Mexico City now stands. The Aztecs welcomed the Spanish as guests and considered the Spanish leader, Hernando Cortés, a god. Cortés captured and killed the Aztec leader, Montezuma. War broke out, and Cortés and his soldiers barely escaped. They returned later with a stronger force and conquered the city. Mexico became a Spanish colony. The natives were poor but they accepted Spanish rule until the late 1700s when the king of that time tried to gain even more power.

The Mexicans, led by Miguel Hidalgo y Costilla, first rebelled against Spanish rule in 1810, but they were unsuccessful. In 1821, the Spaniards signed a treaty granting the Mexicans their independence. Shortly afterward, the Mexican General Santa Anna seized control of the country. American settlers in Texas (then part of Mexico) broke away from Mexico and soon joined the United States. The Mexican War broke out between the United States and Mexico in 1846. Mexico lost the war and signed a treaty giving up half of its territory, but it later received $15 million from the U.S. for the Gadsden Purchase.

Santa Anna fled from Mexico in 1855 during a revolt. A native, Benito Juárez, became the country's new leader. Opposing a new democratic constitution of 1857, landowners and church leaders sought aid from France. With French military backing, an Austrian nobleman named Maximilian was crowned emperor of Mexico in 1864. When French troops withdrew, Maximilian was captured in 1867 and executed by Juárez, who became president again.

After Juárez, there was a period of dictatorship that lasted more than 30 years. Francisco Madero started another revolution in 1910 that led to a republican form of government. Mexican artists such as Diego Rivera and José Clemente Orozco helped lead the revolution.

Today, the government of Mexico is divided into three branches. The president is elected for one six-year term. The legislature consists of a Senate and a Chamber of Deputies. The Mexican Supreme Court forms the judicial branch of the government.

▶ ▶ ▶ ▶ **FIND OUT MORE** ◀ ◀ ◀ ◀
Alamo; Aztecs; Cortés, Hernando; Hildalgo Y Costilla, Miguel; Juárez, Benito; Maya; Mexican War; Mexico City

MEXICO CITY

Mexico City is the capital and largest city of Mexico. It is built on the site of an ancient Aztec city. Mexico City's altitude, 7,800 feet (2,377 m) above sea level, makes it the highest major city in the world. Wide avenues and flowing fountains add to the beauty of Mexico City, where operas and folklore ballets are often presented. Ancient and modern paintings and sculptures fill the city's museums and galleries. The great Diego Rivera's *murals* (wall paintings) at the National Palace show many scenes in the history of Mexico. Public buildings share in the artistic glory of Mexico, with murals painted on many of their walls. Aztec art designs decorate the modern subway.

The University of Mexico is located in a spectacular university city. Large and colorful ceramic murals brighten the outside walls of some of its buildings. The National Museum of Anthropology has displays of ancient native culture, and the Museum of Flora and Fauna shows exotic plants and animals from all over Mexico. Chapultepec Castle is the home of the National Museum of History.

▲ Aztec farmers grew vegetables on reed platforms called *chinampas*. These were built in a lake and were covered with fertile mud.

QUIZ
1. How many states are there in the United States of Mexico?
2. Which artist's murals decorate the palace in Cuernavaca?
3. What is the Mexican unit of currency?
4. What is Mexico's average year-round temperature?
5. Which is Mexico's most important agricultural product: wheat, rice, or corn?
(Answers on page 1792)

▲ A view of Mexico City from Chapultapec Park. The city suffers from pollution and traffic congestion.

MICHELANGELO BUONARROTI (1475–1564)

Some of the greatest achievements in art during the Renaissance were made by Michelangelo. He was both a painter and an architect, but his first love was sculpture. He thought of sculpture as the making of people—cutting solid, human figures from hard stone.

The statue of *Moses*, illustrated below, shows how Michelangelo gave life to his "men of stone." According to the Bible, Moses was the leader of the Hebrews, and the person chosen by God to go up Mt. Sinai and receive the Law (Ten Commandments) from God. In Michelangelo's statue, Moses has just come down from the mountain. He has turned his head and seen the Hebrews worshiping a golden calf instead of God. Moses, ashamed, is getting ready to break the stone tablets of the Law.

▲ A self-portrait of Michelangelo. Although interested in sculpting huge marble statues, his artistic genius spanned painting also.

The Aztec capital, Tenochtitlán, where modern Mexico City stands, was built on an island surrounded by lakes. Hernando Cortés, the Spanish conqueror, captured the city in 1521, and it became the capital of the Spanish colony of New Spain. The Spanish built many handsome structures, including a cathedral. "La Catedral" is the oldest cathedral on the North American continent.

Mexico City was taken by the Americans in 1847 during the Mexican War and by the French in 1863. Mexican patriots recaptured Mexico City in 1867, and it has since remained the capital and major city of Mexico.

In 1985, it suffered a major earthquake, which caused extensive damage both to buildings and to people. More than 4,000 people died.

▶ ▶ ▶ ▶ **FIND OUT MORE** ◀ ◀ ◀ ◀
Aztecs; Cortés, Hernando;
Juárez, Benito; Mexican War; Mexico

▼ *Moses*, a marble figure sculpted by Michelangelo—one of the inspired leaders of the Italian Renaissance, whose life was devoted to art.

Can you see Moses getting ready for action? His expression is one of concentration. His leg is pulled back. His hand reaches across his lap to the tablets. The beard being pulled back and the heavy drapery over the knee give a feeling of tension—a feeling that something is about to happen. Moses' strong body seems to be made of real flesh and blood. Michelangelo had spent many years studying the human body and how it works. Can you see how his knowledge revealed itself in the statue of Moses? Michelangelo created a powerful body for Moses to show the greatness and power of Moses' spirit and character.

Michelangelo was born in Caprese, Italy. His family moved to Florence, a city-state ruled by the Medici family. Michelangelo first studied painting but soon switched to sculpture. Lorenzo the Magnificent, head of the Medici family, was so pleased with Michelangelo's art that he brought him to live and work at the Medici palace.

When Lorenzo died, Michelangelo went to Rome where he sculpted the *Pietà* (a statue of Mary with the crucified Christ across her lap). At the age of 26, he returned to Florence and won the right to carve the "Giant," which was the name people had given to a damaged, 18-foot (5.4-m) slab of marble. No one thought it possible to carve a statue from it, using the entire piece of stone. But Michelangelo carved his great statue of *David*, the slayer of Goliath, from the "Giant."

In 1505, Pope Julius II asked Michelangelo to design a huge tomb. The *Moses* statue was to have been part of it, but the tomb was never completed. The Pope also asked Michelangelo to paint *frescoes* on the enormous ceiling of the Sistine Chapel in the Vatican. Michelangelo created hundreds of giant figures on the wet plaster, showing the creation of the world and hundreds of biblical characters and events. He worked for four years, lying on his back in a cramped position at the top of a 60-foot (18-m) scaffold. The light was dim.

▲ **Michelangelo designed the magnificent dome of St. Peter's Basilica in Rome. It has two galleries, and beneath it is the High Altar.**

His arms ached. Plaster and paint dripped into his eyes. He became ill several times, but he kept working and completed the magnificent frescoes in 1512.

Pope Julius II died in 1513, but his tomb was not finished until 1545. Two other great figures that Michelangelo intended to feature alongside his *Moses* sculpture were of slaves, one in chains, one dying. These are now in museums in Paris, France, and Florence, Italy. In 1536, Michelangelo painted a fresco for the wall behind the altar of the Sistine Chapel. Called the *Last Judgment*, it shows Christ ruling the world. In 1547, Michelangelo was made chief architect of the Church of St. Peter in Rome. He designed its great dome, although architects later altered his designs for the rest of the building.

Michelangelo had tremendous energy, and art was his whole life. In addition to being a sculptor, painter, and architect, he was a poet, expressing in words the same emotions that his other artistic work reveals.

▶ ▶ ▶ ▶ **FIND OUT MORE** ◀ ◀ ◀ ◀
Architecture; Art History; Medici Family; Painting; Renaissance; Sculpture

▲ **This is Michelangelo's famous marble statue of *David*. The artist finished this work in 1504, at the age of 29.**

Among Michigan's most interesting features are the shifting sand dunes that line the shores of Lake Michigan. The biggest is Sleeping Bear Dune, a 600-foot (183-m)-high hill of sand near Glen Arbor. This is the largest shifting sand dune in the world. The sand is so fine that the dune can be used as a ski run.

MICHIGAN

"If you seek a pleasant peninsula, look about you." This sentence, translated from Latin, is the motto of the state of Michigan.

Michigan actually has two peninsulas. One is the Upper (northern) Peninsula. The other, more than twice as large, is the Lower (southern) Peninsula. Each of these two parts of Michigan is almost surrounded by the water of the Great Lakes. Our word "Michigan" comes from a Native American word meaning "big lake." The Straits of Mackinac separate the two parts. A bridge, 5 miles (8 km) long, crosses the straits. The middle section of the bridge is 200 feet (60 m) above the water.

The Land and Climate

The Upper Peninsula has Lake Superior on its northern coast. Lake Michigan and a little of Lake Huron form its southern coast. A narrow, winding strip of water separates Michigan from Canada on the northeast. Michigan's neighbor on the southwest land side is Wisconsin.

The Upper Peninsula is twice the size of the state of Massachusetts. But only a small number of Michigan's people live in this area. It is difficult to earn a living there. The soil is poor, and the forests were almost all cut down by loggers or lumberjacks years ago. The lumberjacks left no seed trees standing. The forests took a long time to grow again. Mines in the peninsula offer a few jobs. But copper ore is no longer mined. Some iron ore is mined, but the iron industry does not need a very large number of workers. The Upper Peninsula is visited by many people who enjoy a rugged out-of-doors life. The peninsula has plenty of open country and wonderful places for woodland camping. There are lakes and streams for fishing, boating, and, if you don't mind cold water, swimming.

The western half of the Upper Peninsula is highland, with ranges of hills. The land in the east is low and swampy in places. Henry Wadsworth Longfellow's story-poem, *The Song of Hiawatha*, is set in the eastern part of the Upper Peninsula. "The scene of the poem is among the Ojibwas on the southern shore of Lake Superior," wrote Longfellow. The hero, Hiawatha, launched his canoe from Michigan's Tahquamenon River.

The Lower Peninsula of Michigan is sometimes called the "Mitten." On the map, it looks like a mitten. Lakes Huron, Saint Clair, and Erie are on the eastern coast. Canada is just across the rivers that connect these lakes. Lake Michigan is on the west coast of the Lower Peninsula. Indiana and Ohio lie to the south.

The northern part of the Lower Peninsula is a broad, flat tableland. The tableland slopes down toward the lakes that border it. Much of the region is woodland and is dotted with many small lakes. But where forests have been cut down, there are open patches of wasteland.

◀ **Large cherry crops are grown beside Lake Michigan.**

Most of the people in Michigan live in the southern part of the Mitten. All of the state's big cities are in this region, including the capital, Lansing. The area also has some of the best agricultural land in the state. Cattle, pigs, and poultry are raised. Dairy farming is important. The chief field crops are corn, sugar beets, potatoes, dry beans, soybeans, hay, and wheat. Much fruit is grown along the Lower Peninsula's Lake Michigan shore. Apples, cherries, pears, and peaches grow in big orchards.

▲ The Mackinac Bridge, linking Mackinaw city (Upper Peninsula) with St. Ignace city (Lower Peninsula). It is one of the world's longest suspension bridges. It spans 3,800 feet (1,160m).

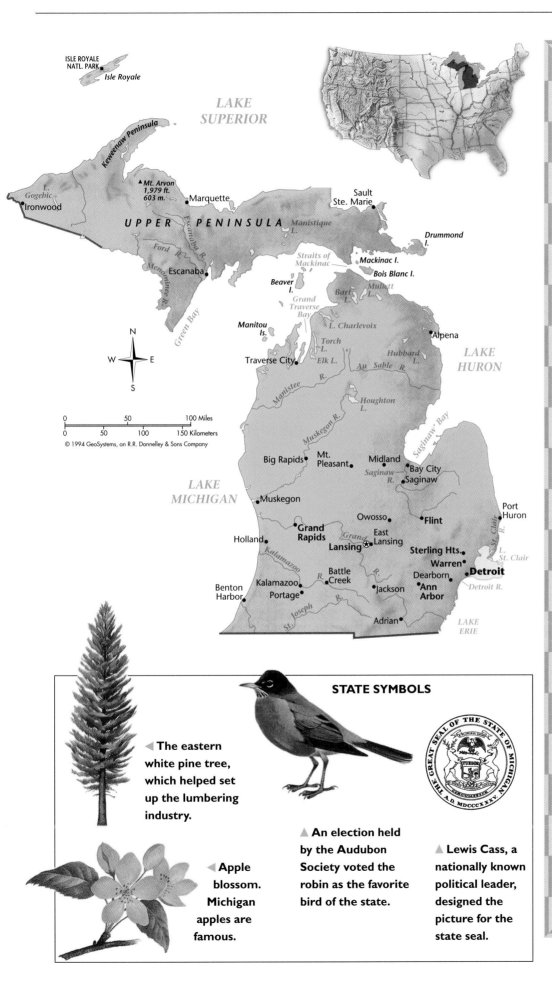

ISLE ROYALE
NATL. PARK
Isle Royale

LAKE SUPERIOR

Keweenaw Peninsula

▲ Mt. Arvon
1,979 ft.
603 m.

• Marquette

L. Gogebic
• Ironwood

U P P E R   P E N I N S U L A

• Sault
Ste. Marie

Manistique L.

Escanaba R.
Ford R.

• Escanaba

Menominee R.

Green Bay

Drummond I.

Straits of Mackinac

Mackinac I.

Bois Blanc I.

Beaver I.

N
W   E
S

Grand Traverse Bay

Bart L.
Mullett L.

Manitou Is.

L. Charlevoix

Torch L.

• Alpena

0   50   100 Miles
0   50   100   150 Kilometers
© 1994 GeoSystems, an R.R. Donnelley & Sons Company

• Traverse City

Elk L.

Hubbard L.

Au Sable R.

LAKE HURON

Manistee R.

Houghton L.

Muskegon R.

Saginaw Bay

LAKE MICHIGAN

• Big Rapids

• Mt. Pleasant

• Midland

Saginaw R.

• Bay City
• Saginaw

• Muskegon

• Owosso

• **Flint**

• Port Huron

St. Clair R.

• **Grand Rapids**

Grand R.

• East Lansing

• **Lansing** ✪

• Holland

Kalamazoo R.

• Sterling Hts.
• **Warren**
• Dearborn

• **Detroit**

L. St. Clair

• Battle Creek

• Jackson

• **Ann Arbor**

Detroit R.

• Benton Harbor
• Kalamazoo
• Portage

St. Joseph R.

• Adrian

LAKE ERIE

MICHIGAN

Capital
Lansing (127,321 people)

Area
58,216 square miles
(150,768 sq. km)

Population
9,265,000 people
Rank: 8th

Statehood
January 26, 1837
(26th state admitted)

Principal river
Grand River

Highest point
Mount Curwood:
1,980 feet (604 m)
in Upper Peninsula

Largest city
Detroit (1,027,979
people; seventh largest
city in U.S.)

Motto
*Si Quaeris Peninsulam
Amoenam Circumspice*
("If you seek a pleasant
peninsula, look about
you")

Song
"Michigan, My Michigan"

Famous people
Robet Jarvik, George
Custer, Thomas Dewey,
Edna Ferber, Henry Ford,
Magic Johnson, Madonna

STATE SYMBOLS

◀ The eastern
white pine tree,
which helped set
up the lumbering
industry.

◀ Apple
blossom.
Michigan
apples are
famous.

▲ An election held
by the Audubon
Society voted the
robin as the favorite
bird of the state.

▲ Lewis Cass, a
nationally known
political leader,
designed the
picture for the
state seal.

1687

▲ **The Renaissance Center. It includes Detroit's highest building, a circular 73-story hotel, 750 feet (229 m) tall.**

▲ **The Menominee tribe attracted fish with flaming torches, then speared the catch as they surfaced.**

The Great Lakes have an important effect on the climate of Michigan. In the fruit-growing region, cold breezes from Lake Michigan keep the tree buds from forming too soon in the early spring. When the lake finally warms up, the danger of frost has passed.

In summer, the lakes help to keep Michigan cool. But they also make the warm season longer. As winter nears, the land becomes cold more quickly than the water. Winds from the Great Lakes, therefore, still warm the land in late fall. Winters in Michigan are fairly cold. Snows are heaviest in the Upper Peninsula.

History

The Ojibwas (Ojibways) mentioned by Longfellow were a major tribe of Native Americans in Michigan. Other tribes were the Ottawa, Menominee, and Potawatomi.

French missionary-priests and fur traders were the first Europeans to visit Michigan. Michigan's earliest permanent settlement was a mission founded by Father Jacques Marquette in 1668. At the mission, Father Marquette gathered the local people together to teach them Christianity. Several forts and trading posts were established by the French in both the Upper and Lower peninsulas. In 1701, Antoine de la Mothe Cadillac, a French army officer, built Fort Pontchartrain, which later grew into the city of Detroit.

Britain defeated France in the French and Indian War, which ended in 1763. But the British were driven out of the region during the Revolutionary War. Michigan became a state of the Union in 1837.

Michigan had by this time become an important lumber area. Big steam sawmills were built. Thousands and thousands of tree trunks were fed to the whirling saws. The mills turned the logs into timbers for ships and houses. Before long, much of Michigan was a dreary wasteland of stumps. The mining industry brought much wealth to the state in the late 1800s. For many years, half of all American copper came from Michigan. Iron ore was also found there in large quantitites. Even today, Michigan is second only to Minnesota in mining iron ore.

People at Work in Michigan

The principal industry in Michigan today is manufacturing. The most important product is automobiles (and their parts). The American automobile industry grew up in the city of Detroit, which is known as the *Automobile Capital of the World* and *Motor City*. Other major products manufactured in Michigan are machinery, metal goods, steel, and chemicals. The other principal industry in Michigan is agriculture.

Tourism is an important business in the state. Crowds go to Detroit and Flint to see automobiles being made. Dearborn is the birthplace of the American automobile manufacturer Henry Ford. It is also the site of Greenfield Village, a series of American historical buildings that Ford collected and restored. Its exhibits deal with American industrial history and life in the 1700s and 1800s.

Michigan is best known as a busy industrial state. But it is also a lively cultural center with many libraries and museums, including the famous Detroit Institute of Arts. It was built in 1885, and its collection of paintings and sculptures includes work by the Mexican artist Diego Rivera. The impressive scenery of Michigan is preserved in several national forests. Its national park, Isle Royale, has the largest herd of great-antlered moose in the United States.

▶ ▶ ▶ ▶ **FIND OUT MORE** ◀ ◀ ◀ ◀
Dairy Farming; Dairy Products; Ford, Henry; French and Indian War; Fur; Great Lakes; Longfellow, Henry Wadsworth; Marquette, Jacques and Joliet, Louis; Ojibwas

⚙ MICROFILM

Storing books, magazines, and other papers has become a serious problem in libraries and offices. These materials take up a lot of space and can be completely destroyed by fires or floods. Microfilming can put an end to these difficulties. Microfilming is a way of photographing papers and recording their contents on very small pieces of film. The film is then stored in labeled metal boxes. These boxes take up only about 5 percent of the space that printed material does. Microfilming also keeps the information safe from fire and water damage.

Special cameras are used to photograph printed material on microfilm. Images of the pages are printed one after another on the film. The images are so small that they cannot be read clearly without magnification. The film can be read by inserting it into a desk projector, which operates like a slide projector. The copy is projected onto a screen at normal size or one and a half times the normal size.

Perhaps your local library has materials on microfilm, such as newspaper or magazine articles. Ask the librarian to help you use the machine.

▶ ▶ ▶ ▶ **FIND OUT MORE** ◀ ◀ ◀ ◀
Library; Photography

🖼 MICRONESIA

Scattered over the southwest Pacific ocean are many small islands that are often grouped together under the name Micronesia ("little islands"). The Micronesians engage mainly in fishing and farming today. But the ruins of stone fortifications on Ponape, one of the Federated States of Micronesia, may be the remains of the buildings of an ancient people.

The Micronesian islands lie north of the equator and east of the Philippine Islands (see the map with the article on PACIFIC ISLANDS). There are more than 3,000 Micronesian islands. They include more than 1,500 square miles (3,800 sq. km) of land spread over an area of ocean greater than the area of the continental United States. Micronesia is part of a larger group of Pacific islands known as Oceania. The two other groups in Oceania are Melanesia ("black islands") and Polynesia ("many islands").

Micronesia is composed of several *archipelagoes,* or clusters of islands. Many of the Micronesian islands are coral *atolls.* An atoll is a ring-shaped coral reef, or ridge, that surrounds a *lagoon.* A lagoon is a shallow body of water, like a pond. A shallow channel often leads across the reef to the open sea beyond. Two of the most famous of these atolls, both of them in the Marshall Islands, are Bikini and Eniwetok, where the United States carried out nuclear tests.

The Mariana Islands and some of the Carolines rise from sea level to form tall volcanic mountain peaks. The scenery of Micronesia is varied and beautiful. There are lush forests

▲ **This machine is used for reading microfilm. It greatly magnifies the words on the microfilm. The next time you have a report to write or information to find, you might find that viewing microfilm on a projector is helpful.**

▼ **The map shows the areas of Micronesia ("little islands"), Melanesia ("black islands"), and Polynesia ("many islands").**

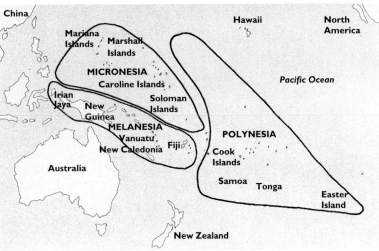

MICRONESIA				
Country, Territory or Association	Status	Area sq. miles (sq. km)	Population	Capital
Belau	Free Association with the U.S.	192 (497)	12,800	Koror
Bonin Islands	Part of Japan	40 (104)	1,000	Omura
Federated States of Micronesia (Caroline Islands, Kosrae, Ponape, Truk, and Yap)	Free association with the U.S.	279 (723)	109,900	Kolonia on Pohnpei
Guam	U.S. Territory	212 (549)	132,000	Agana
Kiribati	Independent 1979	281 (728)	71,000	Tarawa
Northern Mariana Islands	Commonwealth of the Northern Marianas	184 (477)	23,300	Saipan
Marshall Islands	Free association with the U.S.	70 (181)	45,600	Majuro
Nauru	Independent 1968	8 (21)	9,000	Nauru
Tuvalu	Independent 1978	9½ (25)	9,000	Fongafale
Wake Island	U.S. Territory	3 (8)	305	—

Kiribati

Nauru

Tuvalu

and thick mangrove swamps, black sandy beaches, and rocky islands. All of the islands are tropical. Average temperatures range between 70° and 80° F (21°C and 26°C). Micronesia has a long rainy and stormy season—from May to December.

The people of eastern Micronesia are usually tall with light skin. In the western islands, the people are smaller and darker skinned. Micronesians are mainly Christians. They live in small villages of palm-thatched houses. Fishing is their major activity. Coconuts are the chief crop.

Micronesia was visited by the Portuguese explorer Ferdinand Magellan in 1521. After that time, the islands were colonized by Spain, Germany, Great Britain, and Japan. Much of Micronesia was the scene of bitter battles during World War II. After the war, the United Nations gave as a trust territory to the United States the Carolines, Marshall, and Mariana Islands (except for Guam, which was already a U.S. possession). Tuvalu, formerly the Ellice Islands, and Kiribati, formerly the Gilbert Islands, and Nauru, a small island west of Kiribati, are independent nations.

In 1975, the Commonwealth of the Northern Marianas was formed from part of the Mariana Islands, with a status similar to that of Puerto Rico. Under a special agreement with the United States in 1980, the Marshall Islands, the Palau Islands, and the Federated States of Micronesia became self-governing units and no longer trust territories. The Palau Islands declared themselves the Republic of Belau in 1981. Any of these so-called "states" can become fully independent at any time, though the United States would retain military-base rights until 1998.

▶▶▶▶ **FIND OUT MORE** ◀◀◀◀
Pacific Islands

☼ MICROPROCESSOR

It seems hard to imagine that the amount of information stored on your home computer would have required a houseful of computer equipment in the 1950s! Why should that be?

The answer lies in the development of the microprocessor, also called the central processing unit (CPU) of a computer. This is the control center and electronic calculator of a computer. It contains the circuitry needed to carry out program instructions.

The first modern computers, built in the 1940s, were large and bulky. Engineers built computers with tubes and wires. The CPUs would have had thousands of such components.

It became obvious that computer manufacturers would have to *miniaturize* these components if ordinary people were ever to afford computers. The breakthrough came in the early 1970s when the U.S. Intel Corporation developed the *microchip*.

The microchip is a small silicon chip containing an *integrated circuit*. It is the most important and delicate part of a computer's equipment, containing hundreds of thousands of individual electronic components. The silicon chip is sealed inside a black plastic block with metal contacts on its sides, so that it can connect with other computer components.

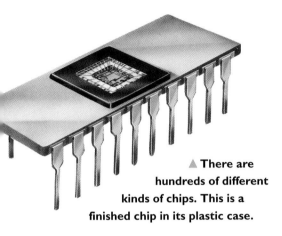

▲ **There are hundreds of different kinds of chips. This is a finished chip in its plastic case.**

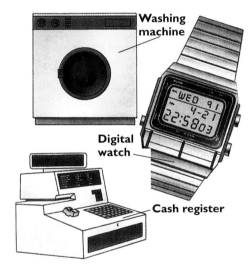

Washing machine

Digital watch

Cash register

▲ **Microprocessors are in many products.**

The computer terms *hardware* and *software* apply especially to microprocessors. The hardware is the microprocessor's equipment used in the normal running of the computer. This includes elements such as the clock, arithmetic/logic unit, and internal memory. The software is the set of related instructions stored in memory and used to control the microprocessor.

▶▶▶▶ **FIND OUT MORE** ◀◀◀◀
Computer; Silicon

⚙ MICROSCOPE

There is a wonderful device that lets you see very tiny things. It opens up a whole new world of things you cannot see with your eyes alone. It is called a *microscope. Micro* means "small" in Greek and *scope* means "to see." The simplest kind of microscope is an ordinary magnifying glass, which has only one lens. If you read this page with a magnifying glass, the words look larger when you hold the glass a certain distance from the page. But a magnifying glass would be of no use to you if you wanted to see all the details of a hair from your head. To see these ordinarily invisible details, you would need a *compound* microscope.

Compound Microscopes

The main parts of a compound microscope are the *base*, *arm*, and *tube*. The tube contains two kinds of lenses. The lens at the bottom of the tube, close to the object that is to be viewed, is called the *objective*. One kind of microscope has a rotating *mount* that holds several objective lenses, each with a different magnifying power. The top of the tube has an eyepiece lens. The bottom of the arm of the microscope is attached to the base. The top of the arm holds the tube.

The base of the microscope has a platform called the stage, on which the *specimen*—the object to be viewed—is placed. The stage has a small hole in it. The hole allows light to be reflected on the specimen from a mirror mounted on the base or from an electric light in the microscope.

To view a specimen, such as a hair, through a microscope, you place the specimen on a small glass strip, called a *slide*. Another glass strip, called a

Eyepiece lens
Tube
Focusing knob
Mount
Objective lens
Stage
Condenser lens
Mirror

▲ **A modern optical microscope has several objective lenses attached to a mount so that it can work at various magnifications. A condenser lens below the specimen table concentrates light reflected from a mirror.**

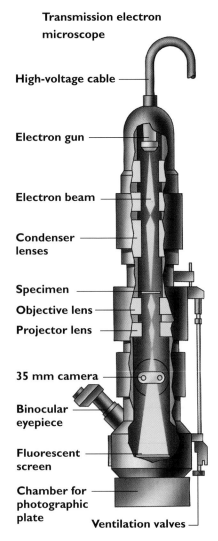

Transmission electron microscope

High-voltage cable

Electron gun

Electron beam

Condenser lenses

Specimen

Objective lens

Projector lens

35 mm camera

Binocular eyepiece

Fluorescent screen

Chamber for photographic plate

Ventilation valves

▲ Electrons from an electron gun are passed through the item being observed to a fluorescent screen. A magnifier enlarges the image.

cover glass, is then placed over the specimen. Some specimens are stained so that they will be easier to see. When a slide is placed on the stage, you look through the *eyepiece* to view the specimen. You *focus*, or get a sharp image, by turning a *coarse adjustment knob* on the arm of the microscope, and then turning a *fine adjustment knob*. The knobs move the tube up and down to place the objective lens at the correct viewing distance from the specimen.

When you look through a microscope, you see a specimen that has been magnified first by the objective lens and then again by the eyepiece lens. If the objective lens magnified the specimen 50 times, and the eyepiece lens magnified the objective image 10 times, the image you see is 500 times larger than the specimen looks to the naked eye. The best compound microscopes can make an object look 2,000 or more times larger than its real size.

The compound microscope was probably invented by Zacharias Janssen, a Dutch eyeglass maker, in about 1590. The first person to see single-celled animals through a microscope was Anton van Leeuwenhoek, who also lived in Holland. Made in 1677, this was one of the first of thousands of scientific discoveries made possible by the microscope.

Pictures of specimens in a microscope can be taken by a process called *photomicrography*. In this process, a camera is mounted directly above the eyepiece. The camera usually does not contain a lens, because the microscope itself acts as the camera's lens system.

Electron Microscopes

The most advanced and most powerful kind of microscope is the *electron* microscope. Very tiny things, such as viruses, may be magnified a million times in an electron microscope! An electron microscope uses beams of electrons, instead of light rays, to "visualize" an object. The "lenses" of an electron microscope are magnetic. They focus the electronic beams in the same way the glass lenses of a compound microscope focus light beams. The image produced by an electron microscope is recorded on photographic film or projected on a screen.

▶▶▶▶ **FIND OUT MORE** ◀◀◀◀
Eye; Glasses; Lens; Light; Photography; Telescope

⚙ MICROWAVES

If your family has a microwave oven, you will know that it can be used to cook food much more quickly than in a normal oven.

Microwaves are types of radio waves. But they have a much shorter wavelength than other radio waves. The longest (lowest-frequency) radio waves have wavelengths of about 60 miles (100 km). Microwaves are high frequency radio waves. The wavelengths of microwaves are about 1/25 inch (1 mm) to 12 inches (30 cm) long.

Microwaves are a form of *electromagnetic radiation*. Other radio waves are also forms of electromagnetic radiation, as are, for example, light and X rays.

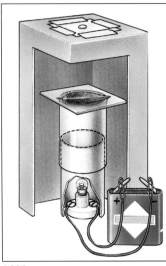

LEARN BY DOING

To make a simple microscope, cut a hole in a piece of cardboard and tape some clear film over it. A drop of water over the hole will act as a lens to magnify objects. Take two cardboard tubes; split one from top to bottom and fit it over the other one tightly. Place an object on a piece of glass on top of the tubes and move the tubes up or down until the object is in focus through your lens. A light bulb will help you to see the object.

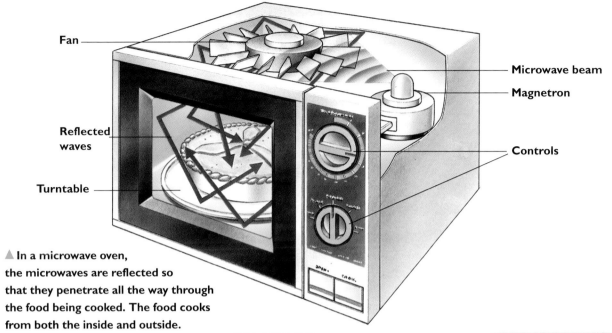

Fan

Reflected waves

Turntable

Microwave beam

Magnetron

Controls

▲ **In a microwave oven, the microwaves are reflected so that they penetrate all the way through the food being cooked. The food cooks from both the inside and outside.**

Electromagnetic radiation transports energy from one place to another. Light is a form of energy: If you go out into the sunshine you can not only see the light, you can feel it as heat. What is happening is that the *photons* of the light are making the molecules in your skin *vibrate* (move backward and forward). The faster the molecules of a substance—your skin, or any other substance—vibrate, the hotter the substance is.

The microwaves in a microwave oven heat foods in the same way. The microwaves make the molecules of water, sugar, and fat in the food vibrate, and this means that the food as a whole heats up. The microwaves are produced by an electrically powered device called a *magnetron*. Microwaves are blocked by the metal walls of the oven, but pass through a cooking dish made of glass, pottery, paper, wood, or plastic. Food inside the dish heats up and cooks, even though the dish stays cool. Metal dishes should not be used in a microwave oven.

▶▶▶▶ **FIND OUT MORE** ◀◀◀◀
Energy; Heat and Cold; Light; Radar; Radiation; Radio; Wave

MIDAS

The myths and legends of ancient Greece tell about a great king named Midas. He ruled the country of Phrygia in Asia Minor. The god of wine, Dionysus, gave Midas the ability to turn everything he touched into gold. Unfortunately, this included his food and wine. Even his little daughter turned into a golden statue when he touched her. Desperate, he begged Dionysus to take back the wish. Dionysus told him to bathe in a nearby river. Midas jumped into the river and broke the spell. Ever since, according to the legend, that river has contained sands of gold.

Another legend says that Midas was once asked to judge a music contest between the gods Pan and Apollo. Midas chose Pan as the winner. Apollo, in a fury, changed Midas's ears into the ears of a donkey. Midas wore a turban to hide the ears, and only his barber knew the secret. One day the barber, unable to keep quiet, dug a hole in the ground and whispered the secret into it. Then all the reeds growing there whispered the story to everyone who passed.

▶▶▶▶ **FIND OUT MORE** ◀◀◀◀
Mythology

▲ **Apollo, the god of music, gives Midas donkey ears in revenge for being rejected.**

WHERE TO DISCOVER MORE

Asimov, Isaac. *How Did We Find Out About Microwaves?* New York: Walker & Co., 1989.

White, Jack R. *The Invisible World of the Infrared.* New York: Dodd, Mead & Co., 1984.

MIDDLE AGES

The years between the end of the Western Roman Empire and the beginning of the Renaissance are known as the Middle Ages (about A.D. 476–1450). The first half of this period is called the "Dark Ages." During the 400s, tribes of people lived in northern Europe. These people were being attacked by Huns (tribes from the East) and being pushed across the borders of the Roman Empire. They came in huge numbers, escaping from the Huns and at the same time fighting the Romans for a place to live. The Roman Empire could not stand up against these invaders. It was overrun by tribes called the Franks, Goths, Visigoths, Ostrogoths, Alemani, Burgundians, Jutes, Teutons, Angles, Saxons, Lombards, Avars, Magyars, and Bulgars. The northern invaders were good warriors, but lacked the skills or civilization to keep the Roman Empire going.

Village Life
During the next 500 years, the Roman Empire no longer existed, and Europe was an unsafe place. People relied on the protection of a chieftain who was powerful enough to fight off an enemy. These chieftains became rulers or lords of small areas. In return for a lord's protec-

▲ The Angles, Jutes, and Saxons were skilled metalworkers who used iron for tools and weapons. They also used bronze, gold, and silver to decorate items such as this ornate helmet from around the year A.D. 625.

tion, a person would become a *vassal*. Vassals had to promise to serve their lord. Some people were free- men, but others became *serfs*, little better than slaves.

People lived in little huts and cottages clustered close to the big house of their lord. In exchange for protection, the people had to farm their lord's land. Farming was the main way of life for most people. People did not travel much, because it was dangerous and the few roads were bad. They had to stay home and work the land.

Agriculture and the need for protection became the basis for a system of government called *feudalism*. In feudalism, every person had a rank—from serf (the lowest rank) to baron or king. Each person had obligations to people of higher and lower rank. Higher-ranking nobles would give pieces of land to lower-ranking nobles. These people were then required to provide soldiers, arms, or food for nobles of higher rank. In this way, everyone was protected and fed.

The Church
Religious people, called monks and nuns, followed Christian teachings in small groups in abbeys or monasteries. Their three main occupations were work, study, and prayer. Monks kept alive the ancient learning of the past, and most could read and write. The monks ran schools and hospitals, helped the poor, set up libraries, and provided *refuge*, or sanctuary, for people fleeing from enemies.

Monasteries began in Italy and then spread to all parts of western Europe. Wherever monks went, they converted the people to Christianity. By the year 1100, Christianity was the religion of all western Europe. The

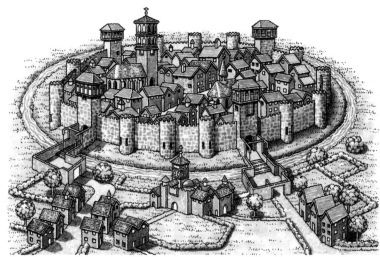

◄ An example of a medieval town, Feurs, in the south of France. The walls protected the town from attack and controlled trade. Tolls could be collected from strangers carrying goods for sale.

Pope in Rome was head of the Church. Bishops were assigned certain areas, and priests were in charge of the local churches. The Church taught that anyone who lived a good life would be rewarded by God. People were afraid of being punished by God if they did wrong. The Church and its teachings helped bring peace to Europe during the Middle Ages. People looked to the Church for education, medicine, and help in hard times. Since everyone in western Europe was Christian, people thought of their religion as *catholic*, universal, a faith for everyone.

The Crusades

In the year 1095, the Pope announced that Europe must free the Holy Land of Palestine (in what is now Israel) from the rule of Arab Muslims. The Europeans thought that the Muslims had no right to rule the Holy Land since they were not Christians. European rulers organized the *Crusades*—long military expeditions to the Holy Land.

The crusaders who went to seize the Holy Land found that the Arabs had built a great civilization. The crusaders admired the Arabs' beautiful carpets, furniture, and spicy food. They also admired Muslim lit-

erature and philosophy as well as their discoveries in mathematics, astronomy, and medicine. In the end, the crusaders failed to recapture the Holy Land, but they took back to Europe the art, architecture, food, spices, silks, and other products of Muslim civilization.

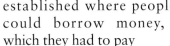

◀ **A rich merchant. Note his fur-lined garments and well-shod feet. Rich men wore their purses on a money belt.**

Towns and Businesses

During the early Middle Ages, traders traveled from one place to another selling their goods. They would meet to exchange goods and get products that their customers wanted. These meetings developed into large trade fairs. Booths displayed pots and pans, leather goods, fabrics, armor and weapons, tools, and many other things.

The trade fairs became towns where traders and craftspeople had their businesses. Guilds were formed. The merchants' guild controlled all the businesses in a town. Each craft—such as weaving, candle making, and baking—had its own guild. People could not practice a craft unless they belonged to a guild. In the late Middle Ages, banks were established where people could borrow money, which they had to pay

One of the most terrible events of the Middle Ages was the Black Death, a form of bubonic plague that wiped out one-third of all the people in Europe. Between 1334 and 1351, it swept from the Middle East through Persia, Russia, Italy, France, England, Germany, and Norway. In London alone, more than 150,000 people died.

▲ **The Church was the seat of learning during the Middle Ages. The *ecclesiastics* (priests, monks, friars etc.) were the only ones who could teach others to read and write. They ran schools and held classes.**

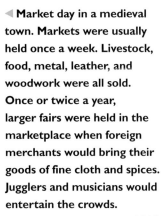

◀ **Market day in a medieval town. Markets were usually held once a week. Livestock, food, metal, leather, and woodwork were all sold. Once or twice a year, larger fairs were held in the marketplace when foreign merchants would bring their goods of fine cloth and spices. Jugglers and musicians would entertain the crowds.**

▶ The Middle Ages were dangerous times. Wars were frequent. Nobles defended their lands by building castles. The local people sought safety inside the castle in time of war. An attacking enemy army would try to knock down the castle walls or starve the defenders into surrender.

WHERE TO DISCOVER MORE

Unstead, R. J. *See Inside a Castle*. New York: Warwick Press, 1986.
Macaulay, David. *Cathedral: The Story of Its Construction*. New York: Houghton Mifflin, 1973.

back with interest. As business grew, towns became larger and stronger. Town councils were set up, and the nobles (on whose lands the towns were located) allowed the towns to govern themselves.

Education

The Church provided the only education during the Middle Ages. Students went to cathedral schools to be taught by master teachers in subjects such as languages, philosophy, mathematics, medicine, and astronomy. Often masters and students formed themselves into a guild, called a *universitas*, and set up rules to guide their schooling. Universities in the Middle Ages had no special buildings. Masters rented rooms, and students sat on the floor. Each student was given a test about halfway through the training or learning. If the test was passed, the student became a *baccalaureus* (advanced student) and was able to be an assistant teacher. After finishing the course of education, the student became a master teacher.

The Arts

Art in the Middle Ages was almost always connected with religion. Architects created giant cathedrals to honor God. Sculptors decorated cathedral walls with statues and carvings of biblical figures. Glassmakers created brilliant stained-glass windows showing scenes and symbols of the Christian religion. Some monks worked on *manuscript illumination* (drawing pictures and designs to illustrate or decorate a book). Artists painted pictures to be hung in churches. Religious plays, called *morality, miracle,* or *mystery plays*, were performed. Church music was sung in Latin by cathedral choirs. Popular songs were sung by everyone and were accompanied by a lute or harp.

The End of the Middle Ages

By the 1500s, the printing press had been invented. More people were able to read and learn. Merchants were traveling throughout the known world, bringing back new products and knowledge. Kingdoms and city-states had developed. Peo-

◀ Stone carvers left their own marks to identify their work. They sometimes carved faces of people they knew on gargoyles and other decorations on churches they built.

ple could now learn about the past through books and begin to explore the world around them. In Europe, the Renaissance had begun.

▶▶▶▶ **FIND OUT MORE** ◀◀◀◀
Art History; Castle; Cathedral; Christianity; City; Crusades; Drama; Education; Feudalism; Gothic Architecture; Guild; Islam; Knighthood; Monastic Life; Pope; Renaissance; Sculpture; Stained Glass

MIDDLE EAST

The Middle East has been called "The Cradle of Civilization." Great empires developed there more than 5,000 years ago. The first farmers, and the first towns, were in the Middle East. We know about these ancient empires because their people left written records. The Sumerians, who lived on land between the Tigris and Euphrates rivers (in what is now Iraq), were the first people to develop written language.

Today, this ancient land has become an area of conflict in a struggle for change—a struggle between old and new, Arab and Jew, Muslim and Christian.

The People
In the Middle East live people of different races, nationalities, cultures, educational levels, and religious sects. Most of the people are Arabs, and most of the Arabs are Muslims, followers of the Islamic religion.

Christians, Jews, and Muslims can be found in almost every Middle Eastern land. For example, Christian Arabs make up about half the population of Lebanon, one of the most troubled of Middle East countries. The modern State of Israel is made up largely of Jewish people who have come to the Middle East from Western and Eastern Europe. Israel's population is 82 percent Jewish, with about 14 percent Arabs. In Turkey and Iran

are many people descended from Indo-Europeans. Most of the Turkish people are Muslims, but not Arabs. They speak Turkish, not Arabic.

The Middle East is not a unified cultural area. Turkey, for instance, long ago cast off many Muslim customs, such as the wearing of veils by women. Israel is influenced much more by Western ideas than its neighbors are. Yet all of these lands (Arabia, Egypt, Iran, Iraq, Israel, Jordan, Lebanon, Syria, and Turkey) are involved in the current problems of the world.

The Land
The Middle East is a land mass forming an important crossroad between Asia, Africa, and Europe. It has coastlines on the Caspian, Black, Mediterranean, Red, and Arabian seas. Great deserts, where nomadic tribes still herd sheep, cover much of the land. Mount Damavand, in northern Iran, is 18,386 feet (5,604 m) high. The Dead Sea in Jordan is the lowest point on Earth—1,320 feet (402 m) below sea level.

Searching for water in their hot, dry lands has influenced much of the people's history and way of life. Since gaining independence in 1948, Israel has made remarkable progress in using modern techniques of conservation to bring fresh water south from the Jordan River. By laying pipelines, Israelis have managed to make

▲ It is the custom for women in many Middle Eastern states to cover their bodies in a long robe. Religion and local laws dictate the rules about this, but usually the lips, arms, and legs are hidden.

Country	Area sq. miles	Area sq. km	Population	Capital
Cyprus*	3,572	9,251	742,000	Nicosia
Egypt	386,662	1,001,449	53,170,000	Cairo
Iran	636,296	1,648,000	56,923,000	Tehran
Iraq	167,925	434,924	17,754,000	Baghdad
Israel	18,019	20,770	4,616,000	Jerusalem
Jordan	37,738	97,740	3,173,000	Amman
Lebanon	4,015	10,400	2,965,000	Beirut
Syria	71,498	185,180	12,113,000	Damascus
Turkey	301,382	780,576	56,941,000	Ankara

*Note: Cyprus has been divided into separate Turkish and Greek Cypriot areas since 1974.

▲ Oil has made some Middle Eastern states very rich, despite their lack of other resources. This refinery is in Saudi Arabia, the largest oil producer in the region.

Very few people agree as to what the Middle East is. Some scholars say it includes countries such as the Sudan, Libya, and other north African states. Others make it a much smaller area, excluding these countries and even Egypt.

the rocky Negev Desert "bloom." Syrian and Jordanian farmers also use water from the Jordan to irrigate their fields. Neither the Arabs nor the Israelis can increase their use of water from the Jordan River without depriving their rivals. The continual struggle over the Jordan River's limited flow is a source of tension.

History

The Middle East has been a target for conquest since ancient times because of its location, culture, and wealth. During the Middle Ages, the Christians of Europe sought to drive the Muslims out of the Holy Land (Palestine). A long series of wars, the Crusades, were fought from the 1000s to the 1200s to capture the Holy Land and the city of Jerusalem for Christianity.

After World War II, a part of Palestine became the Jewish state of Israel. Yet almost a million Arabs lived there. Many Arabs felt that the Western nations, which had voted for the establishment of the State of Israel in the United Nations, had broken their promise of complete self-rule and independence for the Middle Eastern Arabs. Many Palestinian Arabs became refugees, living in camps. Border clashes, acts of sabotage, and outright warfare have been the general state of affairs between Israel and most Arab states. Egypt and Israel signed a peace treaty in 1979, ending about 30 years of war between them. How-

▲ Iranian protesters support the religious revolutionary leader, Ayatollah Khomeini (1900–1989), in 1979 during an anti-U.S.A. demonstration.

ever, elsewhere the terrorism and tensions have continued. In August 1990, Iraq invaded Kuwait. It was the beginning of the Persian Gulf War, which lasted just over six months and involved the sending of a multinational force by the United Nations to liberate Kuwait.

The Middle East is rich in oil, holding more than half of the world's known supply. The Middle East nations with the most oil are Iran, Iraq, and the states of Arabia. Most of the oil is shipped to Japan and European countries; some goes to the United States. The Middle Eastern countries spend much of the money received from the sale of oil to build highways, airports, factories, schools,

▶ Jerusalem is a city sacred to Christians, Jews, and Muslims. Every year thousands of pilgrims visit it. Since 1967, the whole city has been occupied by Israel, whose capital it is.

and hospitals. Also, much money is spent buying weapons.

Some of the countries in the Middle East, such as Egypt and Israel, are ruled by presidents, prime ministers, and elected parliaments. Jordan has a king with limited power over parliament. Other countries have military governments. The Middle East is an area of conflict and instability. This was obviously made worse by the Persian Gulf Crisis, but in 1991, world leaders organized a Middle East conference in Madrid to start working for peace in this troubled area. By 1994, Israelies and Palestinians signed an agreement to live together peacefully.

MIGRATION

Many animals travel at certain times of the year. They leave one area and go somewhere else for part of the year. Later, they return. Migrating animals usually return to the same place each year when it is time to have their young. Birds are the best-known migrating animals, but many

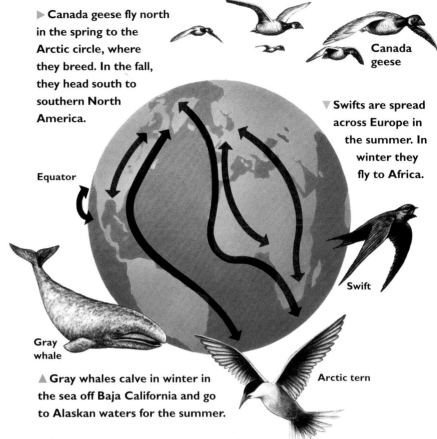

▶ **Canada geese fly north in the spring to the Arctic circle, where they breed. In the fall, they head south to southern North America.**

Canada geese

▼ **Swifts are spread across Europe in the summer. In winter they fly to Africa.**

Equator

Swift

Gray whale

▲ **Gray whales calve in winter in the sea off Baja California and go to Alaskan waters for the summer.**

Arctic tern

other animals migrate, too. Whales, caribou, bats, fish, and seals are migrators. Some insects also migrate.

Mammals

Migrating mammals usually follow the same paths year after year, and they always migrate at the same seasons. Usually mammals migrate in order to find food and water. Caribou, for example, raise their young in the far northern parts of Canada and Alaska. As summer ends, thousands of caribou leave the *tundra* (northern plains) and head for the shelter of forests in the south. Their swift-trotting migrations take them hundreds of miles. In the spring, they return to the tundra.

The American buffalo, or bison, once migrated in enormous herds. They traveled between summer feeding grounds on the northern Great Plains and winter pastures in the lower Mississippi Valley, always using the same trails. The bison, by changing their feeding grounds regu-

▲ **Arctic terns breed in the Arctic summer and fly 11,000 miles (17,500 km) to the Antarctic for the winter.**

Springbok, wildebeast, zebra, and other large African mammals trek long distances from dry areas to wet regions where new plants are growing. These journeys are not as predictable as the seasonal migrations, but they involve some of the largest mass movements of animals on Earth.

▲ Migrating animals, especially birds, often gather in huge numbers. There may be thousands of birds in a migratory flock.

▼ When winter comes to North America, the caribou herds migrate. They leave the bleak Arctic plains for the shelter of the forests further south. Birds such as the snow goose also migrate each year. Lemmings do not migrate. Instead, they make a one-way journey when their numbers become so great they need extra food.

larly, did not overgraze the land. New grass had a chance to grow strong before the herds returned.

Many seals, whales, and other sea mammals are migratory. The Alaska fur seals spend the cold winter months off the coasts of Mexico and Japan. In spring, they swim north through the Pacific Ocean and do not stop until they reach the Pribilof Islands near Alaska. There, the baby seals are born. In winter, thousands of seals go southward again.

Every few years, *lemmings* (small mouselike animals in northern regions) migrate in search of more living space and more food. Thousands of them may travel together, always moving in one direction. They swim across rivers and lakes. Some lemmings may reach the coast, enter the ocean, and swim on and on, eventually drowning from exhaustion.

People have also been migrators. Thousands of years ago, the ancestors of human beings traveled from Africa to all parts of the world. They were hunters and followed the migrating animals north in summer and south in winter to obtain food.

Birds

Every part of the United States has some migrating birds. Most of the bird population east of the Rocky Mountains stays around only during certain seasons. In the fall they leave, and in spring they return to build nests. West of the Rocky Mountains, there are more *resident birds*. Resi-

dent birds do not migrate.

Many migrating birds are able to withstand cold temperatures and can find enough food in winter. This means they do not migrate just to find food or escape the cold. Many scientists think that migration is a habit. Birds probably began to migrate during the ice ages, when the northern regions of the world were much colder than they are now, and they have gone on doing so.

Some birds fly great distances when migrating. North American warblers, for instance, spend the winter in South America. The Arctic tern migrates farther than any other bird. In summer, it lives in the most northern parts of Europe, Siberia, and North America. In winter, it migrates to the most southern area of the world, the Antarctic. An Arctic tern's round trip may be as long as 22,000 miles (35,000 km). Not all birds migrate long distances. Some fly only from fresh water to salt water, or from high mountains to the valleys below.

Many birds fly only at night when they are migrating. If you could shine a big light into the night skies during migratory months, you might see warblers, flycatchers, vireos, orioles, tanagers, and most of the shore birds. Hawks, swallows, ducks, and geese migrate during the day.

How do birds find their way? Why do they travel along certain routes? Nobody knows all the answers. Some scientists think that birds learn to recognize landmarks—certain moun-

Snow goose

Caribou

Gray whales

Lemmings

tains, coastlines, and rivers. Experiments have shown that night-flying birds use the stars to help them.

Migrating birds are born with a *homing instinct*. With this instinct they can tell when to migrate, where to go, and how to return. In experiments, birds have been taken far from their nests and set free. They always return.

Insects and Fish

The migrations of butterflies and some locusts are the best-known examples of insect migration. About 50 kinds of butterflies migrate each autumn. Each year they move to the same places their ancestors used. Some locusts are migratory and fly great distances in search of fresh food.

The salmon is probably the best known of the migratory fish. Unlike birds, these fish migrate only twice during their lives. Their migration is caused by the breeding instinct. Salmon lay their eggs in freshwater rivers and streams. After they lay their eggs, the salmon die. The young then hatch out and swim downstream to the oceans and seas. Later they struggle against currents, rapids, and waterfalls to return to the very place where they were hatched. They lay their eggs, then die, and the process is repeated.

▶ ▶ ▶ ▶ **FIND OUT MORE** ◀ ◀ ◀ ◀
Animal; Animal Movement; Bird;
Bison; Butterflies and Moths;
Fish; Human Being; Insect; Lemming;
Reproduction; Seals and Sea Lions;
Whales and Whaling

MILK

SEE DAIRY PRODUCTS

MILKY WAY

If you have ever looked at the sky on a moonlit night, away from the reflected lights of a city, then you have probably seen the Milky Way. The Milky Way is a faint, shining band of light across the sky.

The Milky Way is a galaxy, a huge collection of billions of stars. The sun is one of these stars. The Milky Way is what astronomers call a *spiral galaxy.* It is shaped something like a spiral wheel. This wheel is at least 100,000 light-years across, but only about 10,000 light-years in thickness. The picture helps to explain why our galaxy looks like a band of light. The dots are the stars of the Milky Way, and the arrows show the position of our sun. From Earth we see only part of the spiral arm in which the sun and its planets are situated. It looks like a continuous faint band of light stretching across the sky, passing through such constellations as Cassiopeia and Perseus. The bulging center of the spiral system contains very old stars. The spiral arms have younger stars.

▶ ▶ ▶ ▶ **FIND OUT MORE** ◀ ◀ ◀ ◀
Astronomy; Star; Sun; Universe

MILNE, A. A. (1882–1956)

The British writer A. A. (Alan Alexander) Milne is known all over the world for his stories about the toy bear Winnie-the-Pooh. Milne was born in London. After studying at Cambridge University, he worked for eight years as an editor for *Punch,* a British humor magazine. He wrote several novels, short stories, and many plays, including *Mr. Pim Passes By.* His autobiography, *It's Too Late Now,* was published in 1939.

◀ The two main populations of monarch butterflies are found in North and South America. Both populations move nearer to the Equator in the fall.

▲ Two views of our galaxy, the Milky Way. The positions of our sun and *solar system* (the planets) are shown by the arrows. The stars are concentrated in one plane, making a whitish band. Light from the center of the Milky Way takes about 27,000 years to reach the earth.

▲ A. A. Milne, the British writer who created the character of the bear Winnie-the-Pooh.

Milne wrote four books for his small son, Christopher Robin. *When We Were Very Young* and *Now We Are Six* are collections of delightful poems about childhood. *Winnie-the-Pooh* and *The House at Pooh Corner* are stories about some very lovable toy animals. Pooh, who belongs to Christopher Robin, is a bear "with a Pleasing Manner but a Positively Startling Lack of Brain." Pooh loves honey ("hunny") more than anything else and often gets into difficulties trying to get more of it. (Pooh often feels it necessary to stop for a "little something" from his hunny jar.) He lives in a forest with his friends—Piglet; the gloomy donkey Eeyore; Owl; Kanga and little Roo; Rabbit; and playful, bouncing Tigger the tiger. Milne's endearing characters, drawn by the British artist Ernest H. Shepard, are fun to read about. Once you have met the "Bear of Very Little Brain," you will never forget him.

▶▶▶▶ **FIND OUT MORE** ◀◀◀◀
Children's Literature

▲ John Milton, English poet and political writer, famous for his epic poems, *Paradise Lost* and *Paradise Regained*.

MILTON, JOHN (1608–1674)

Religion and politics were the major forces in the life of the English poet John Milton. As one of the leaders of the Puritans, a strict Protestant group, he disagreed with many of the practices of the Church of England. He expressed his religious and political convictions in his writings.

John Milton was born in London, England, and was educated at Cambridge University. When he became involved in the growing Puritan movement, he wrote several *pamphlets* (booklets), criticizing the practices of the English church and government. During this period, he wrote two of his most famous prose works: *Areopagitica* (a demand for freedom of the press) and *Of Education*. Milton supported the Puritans

during the English Civil War, and he was active in the Puritan government until the monarchy was restored by the Royalists in 1660.

Milton wrote much of his best poetry after his retirement from public life, although he had become blind by this time. He dictated his works to his daughters, who wrote them down. Although he wrote less serious poems, religion is the major theme in most of his poetry. His long epic poem *Paradise Lost* tells the dramatic story of how Satan, once an angel, rebels against God and persuades Adam and Eve to reject God's commands. *Paradise Regained*, a somewhat shorter epic poem, describes Christ's coming to save mankind from the mistakes of Adam and Eve.

▶▶▶▶ **FIND OUT MORE** ◀◀◀◀
Children's Literature; English History; Literature; Poetry; Puritan

MIMICRY

SEE BUTTERFLIES AND MOTHS, PROTECTIVE COLORING

MINERAL

Many people think a mineral is anything that is neither animal nor vegetable. To a prospector or a miner, a mineral is an *ore*—something found in the earth from which metals or other useful materials can be made. To a physician or a dietitian, minerals are very small amounts of certain metals (such as iron and copper) that are found in foods and are needed by the human body for good health. To a scientist, a mineral is a chemical element or compound found in or on the earth. Gold, iron, quartz, and salt are examples of minerals. Scientists have discovered more than 2,000 minerals. All minerals are solids, except for petroleum, mercury, water, and natural gas.

The Structure of Minerals

The elements that make up any mineral are always the same. Quartz is always made up of the elements silicon and oxygen and nothing more. The gem mineral beryl is always composed of beryllium, aluminum, silicon, and oxygen. Because the elements of a mineral are always the same, scientists say that the mineral has a *constant composition of elements*.

In quartz, there is always one atom of silicon for every two atoms of oxygen. Quartz can never have three atoms of silicon and one of oxygen, or any other combination of silicon and oxygen atoms. Because the amount of each element in a mineral is always the same, scientists say that the mineral has *definite proportions*.

Coal looks like a mineral, but it does not have a constant composition. Its elements are not always the same. Coal is made up of carbon from decaying plants that died hundreds of millions of years ago. Along with the carbon are various amounts of sulfur and some compounds of carbon, hydrogen, and oxygen.

Minerals are almost always *crystalline*. This means that they are made up of crystals. A crystal is a combination of atoms that join together to form a definite, orderly shape. The outer shape of a perfect crystal (one that is not broken) shows the arrangement of the atoms.

Minerals and Rocks

Rocks are not minerals. Rocks are mixtures of minerals that have been formed by heat or pressure in the earth, or by the action of water. A few kinds of rocks, such as marble, are made up of only one mineral.

A pure mineral has a *constant weight*. A rock does not. One cubic inch of any mineral weighs exactly as much as all other cubic inches of the same mineral. The weight of a cubic

Turquoise

Jade

Diamond

Emerald

Lapis lazuli

inch of rock depends on the amounts of light and heavy minerals in the rock. If you weigh two pieces of the same rock, each a cubic inch in size, you will see that their weights differ. The heavier piece contains heavier minerals.

How Minerals Form

At one time in its early history, the Earth was a hot mass of melted substances. All the elements that made up the Earth were liquid. These liquid elements mixed. Some combined chemically, forming compounds. The

▲ The beauty of a mineral may depend on its color, transparency, or luster. Emeralds are an attractive color and transparent. Diamonds owe their beauty to their "fire"—the way they disperse light. The Ancient Egyptians used turquoise in their jewelry. The Chinese favor jade and lapis lazuli.

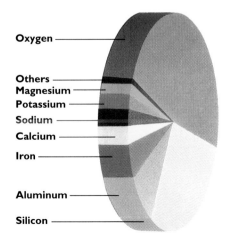

Oxygen

Others
Magnesium
Potassium
Sodium
Calcium
Iron

Aluminum

Silicon

◄ This pie chart shows the various elements, including minerals, found in the Earth's crust. They are shown in the proportions in which they occur.

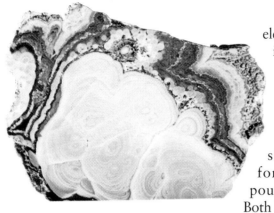

▲ **Malachite and azurite are two ores of copper and are often found in the same piece of rock. Malachite is used for ornamental purposes. A blue pigment comes from azurite.**

elements that combine easily with other elements (such as silicon, aluminum, iron, and oxygen) formed the most compounds. Other elements (such as gold, silver, and platinum) formed very few compounds, or remained pure. Both kinds of elements became minerals.

Metallic and Nonmetallic Minerals

There are two main kinds of minerals, *metallic* and *nonmetallic*. Metallic minerals may be pure metals, such as gold and silver. They may also be compounds containing elements that are metals, such as *galena,* which is composed of lead and sulfur. Nonmetallic minerals contain no metal elements. Quartz is a nonmetallic mineral, because the silicon and oxygen elements are not metals.

▼ **A selection of minerals that show the wide variety of colors and formations.**

Agate

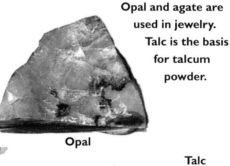

Opal and agate are used in jewelry. Talc is the basis for talcum powder.

Opal

Talc

Calcite

Augite

Yellow serpentine

Naming Minerals

The names of most minerals—they often end in *ite*—are a kind of shorthand way of describing their history. Some are named for scientists who discovered them: Lechatelierite, for example, is named after the French chemist Henry Le Chatelier. Some minerals get their names from the place where they were first found. Labradorite, for example, is named after the Labrador region of northeastern Canada. Other minerals have names made up from the chemical elements that make them up. Sinoite, for example, comes from Si for silicon, N for nitrogen, and O for oxygen. Still other mineral names are so ancient that no one knows their origin. Quartz and feldspar are examples of such minerals.

Identifying Minerals

Minerals can be described by their characteristics. Each mineral has a different set of characteristics. By describing the characteristics of a mineral, you set it apart from others. In this way, you can identify it.

LUSTER. The luster of a mineral is the way it shines when in the light. There are two main kinds of luster, *metallic* and *nonmetallic*. A metallic luster is one that looks like the surface of a metal. The mineral called pyrite, or fool's gold, has a metallic luster.

There are several kinds of nonmetallic lusters. *Adamantine* is the shine such as diamonds have. *Vitreous* luster is like a broken edge of glass. *Resinous* luster is like *resin* (the sap from a tree). *Pearly* luster is the shine such as pearls have. *Silky* luster is like silk. *Dull* describes a surface that has no shine at all.

HARDNESS. Some minerals are harder than others. A harder mineral can scratch a softer one. In 1822, Friedrich Mohs, a German scientist, devised a hardness scale in which he listed 10 minerals from softest (number 1) to hardest (number 10).

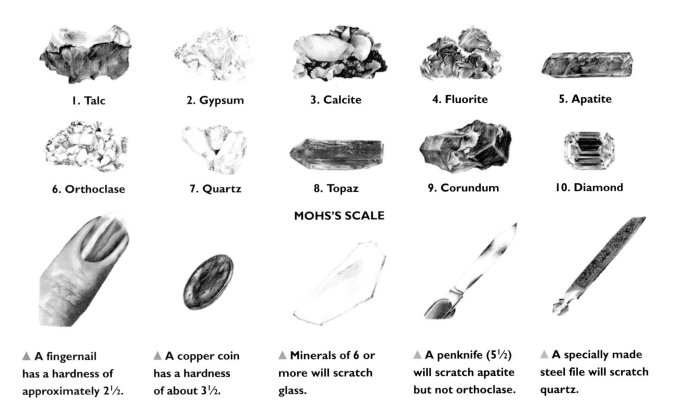

1. Talc   2. Gypsum   3. Calcite   4. Fluorite   5. Apatite

6. Orthoclase   7. Quartz   8. Topaz   9. Corundum   10. Diamond

MOHS'S SCALE

▲ A fingernail has a hardness of approximately 2½.

▲ A copper coin has a hardness of about 3½.

▲ Minerals of 6 or more will scratch glass.

▲ A penknife (5½) will scratch apatite but not orthoclase.

▲ A specially made steel file will scratch quartz.

COLOR. Minerals are found in all colors. The color may be due to light passing through the mineral. Such a mineral is *transparent* if you can see objects through it, as through glass. It is *translucent* if you can see only light, but not objects, through it. Many transparent and translucent minerals are gems. Diamond, ruby, sapphire, emerald, and topaz are some transparent gem minerals. Rose quartz, moonstone, and serpentine are translucent gem minerals. Some minerals are translucent when they are in thick pieces and transparent in thin sheets. Mica is such a mineral. Minerals through which light cannot pass are *opaque*. Their color is due to the way light is reflected from their surface. Gold, copper, and turquoise are opaque minerals.

SPECIFIC GRAVITY. The weight of a mineral is an important characteristic. Its weight is usually called *specific gravity*. Specific gravity is found by comparing the weight of an amount of mineral and the weight of the same volume of pure water.

INDEX OF REFRACTION. When light passes through any substance, the direction in which the light travels is changed. The amount of change is called the *index of refraction* of the substance. Different minerals have different indexes of refraction.

CRYSTAL STRUCTURE. The shape of the crystals that make up each mineral is different, and it is a good way to identify the mineral.

STREAK. The streak of a mineral is the color it has when ground up into a powder. The streak may be quite different from the color seen in a lump of the mineral. For example, lumps of iron ore *(hematite)* may be brown, green, or black, but all have a red-brown streak.

Useful Minerals

There are many useful minerals. Besides those that are valuable gemstones, the most useful minerals are metal ores. Iron is made from hematite, magnetite, and siderite ores. Aluminum comes from bauxite ore. Lead comes from galena ore. Tin is made from cassiterite ore. Nickel

▲ The hardness of minerals can be determined by using Mohs's scale. Mohs selected ten minerals and arranged them in order of hardness. The intervals on the scale are not regular. Although topaz is only seven times as hard as talc, diamond is 40 times as hard as talc.

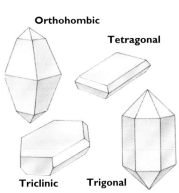

Orthohombic

Tetragonal

Triclinic   Trigonal

▲ Most minerals have regular structures of crystals. The crystal shapes make each mineral type look different.

During the Gold Rush, in the mid-1800s, gold was mined in small amounts by swirling river sands and water in a shallow pan. The heavy gold stays in the pan. The sand is washed away.

▼ A pie chart showing the most important metals mined in the United States (by value in billions of dollars).

Copper $3.77

Gold $2.83

Magnesium $0.47

Silver $0.35

Zinc $0.32

Iron ore $1.72

comes from pentlandite ore. *Asbestos* is not a single mineral, but a soft, silky flexible form of the minerals chrysolite, actinolite, tremolite, amosite, and crocidolite. Asbestos is useful because it will not burn in a fire. Asbestos is light in weight and can be woven into fabrics that will not burn, decay, or be destroyed by strong chemicals. Because asbestos is dangerous to human health, it no longer is used to insulate buildings against heat and sound.

▶▶▶▶ **FIND OUT MORE** ◀◀◀◀
Characteristics of Minerals see
Atom; Chemistry; Crystal;
Element; Gas; Light; Liquid;
Rock; Solid; Weight
Formation of Minerals see
Earth History; Geology; Granite;
Matter; Solar System
Kinds of Minerals see
Diamond; Gem; Gold; Iron and Steel;
Metal; Petroleum; Silver; Water
Uses of Minerals see
Coal; Construction; Fire; Fuel;
Jewelry; Manufacturing;
Mines and Mining

MINES AND MINING

Ever since ancient times, people have been taking out of the earth minerals and other valuable materials, such as gold, silver, diamonds, rubies, copper, iron, sulfur, and coal. When any one of these things is found in an amount large enough to make it worthwhile to be taken out of the earth, it is called *ore*. Digging and washing out ore is called mining. The holes that are dug to get at ores are mines.

A *deposit* is an accumulation of ore. Some kinds of deposits have special names. A long, branching deposit, surrounded by rock, is called a *vein* of ore. Gold and silver may be found in veins. A wide, flat deposit is often called a *bed*. Coal is found in beds. Oil and natural gas deposits are called *wells*.

Prospecting

Searching for ore is called *prospecting*. For thousands of years, prospecting was done by persons (prospectors) who simply wandered around looking for signs of ore. In places where streams, rainwater, or landslides removed some of the earth above an ore deposit, the ore was exposed to the prospector's view—if one came along.

About 150 years ago, *geologists*—scientists who study the Earth—learned how to make maps of the rocks in an area. Miners had noticed that certain kinds of ores usually were in or near certain kinds of rock. With maps to guide them to the proper kinds of rock, prospectors knew where they should dig for ore.

By the end of World War II, almost all the easy-to-find ore deposits had been found. Mining geologists then turned to prospecting with scientific instruments. One of these is the *seismograph*, which records the speed of shock waves traveling through the Earth. The prospector explodes dynamite in holes drilled in the ground. Shock waves from the explosion are recorded by the seismograph. If ore is in the area of the explosion, the speed of waves passing through the deposit will be different from their speed in the surrounding earth.

Prospectors fly instruments over an area in which they think there may be ore. One of these instruments is a *magnetometer*. It measures changes in the Earth's magnetism, which is slightly different around a deposit of iron, nickel, or cobalt ore. A similar instrument is a *gravity meter*, which records changes in the strength of the Earth's gravity. Such changes can tell of the presence of ore deposits. A *scintillation counter* can locate radioactive ores, such as uranium.

After finding a deposit, a mining engineer must decide whether it is ore—a deposit that will be worth digging up. The deposit may be very deep

or embedded in rock that makes mining very difficult, perhaps dangerous, and may be more expensive to dig than the value of the ore itself.

Sometimes the way in which an ore deposit is mined will determine whether it is worth mining. Suppose only 50¢ worth of gold is in every ton of gravel in a riverbed. A lone miner, who can dig and search through only 3 or 4 tons of gravel a day, cannot get more than two dollars for a day's work. But a large dredge that can work through 18,000 tons (18,300 metric tonnes) of gravel a day will make it worthwhile to mine the same gravel.

As more mining methods improve, miners find it worthwhile to mine ore deposits that they would have passed by as too expensive to extract a few years before.

Mining Methods

The three main methods of mining ore are *placer, open-pit,* and *underground.*

In placer mining, miners try to obtain metals that exist in gravel as lumps or grains of pure metal. They use strong jets of water to wash the gravel into a narrow box, or chute, called a *sluice box.* The sluice box has a rough bottom. Water running through the sluice washes away the lighter gravel, leaving the heavier metal on the bottom of the box. Gold is the chief metal mined in this way.

Panning is a kind of placer mining used mainly by prospectors during the gold rush in the 1800s. They scooped up water and sediment from streams into a flat pan. Swirling the water around in the pan would reveal any pieces of gold in the sediment.

▲ An aerial view of Bingham Canyon copper mine, near Salt Lake City, Utah. It also contains a rich deposit of gold and silver. Copper is often dug out with power shovels in steps 40 to 70 feet (12 to 21m) high.

▲ **A powerful excavating machine used to dig out ores, once the topsoil and rock have been removed.**

▶ **The Earth's mineral resources are obtained in many different ways. Large amounts are dredged from rivers, while ores deep below the Earth's surface are reached by tunnels and shafts. When ores are near the surface, the rock is broken up and removed. Building materials are quarried, cut, blasted, from the ground.**

If ore deposits are near the surface, open-pit mining is used. In this kind of mining, the soil and other kinds of earth—called the *overburden*—are dug, or *stripped,* away from the top of the ore deposits. Then large amounts of ore are dug up cheaply by large power shovels. This method is used to mine iron, copper, and aluminum ore and coal. Mining coal from shallow pits is called *strip-mining.*

In underground mining, a wide hole, called a *shaft,* is dug straight down alongside the ore deposit. Then a horizontal tunnel, often called a *crosscut,* is dug from the shaft to the ore. Miners work in a cleared area in the ore called a *stope.* The ore is sent in small cars to the shaft, where it is dumped into a container called a *skip hoist.* The skip, which is like an elevator car, is hoisted to the surface of the earth and dumped. The miners keep digging a

stope, making it longer, as they follow the deposit of ore. When the stope has passed through the ore, or when the stope becomes too long for the miners to work in conveniently, a new one is begun.

Mine Safety

Working underground is dangerous, and in the past many miners were injured or died in accidents due to poor safety regulations. And today, despite vastly improved technology and strict regulations, accidents do happen.

One hazard for early miners was poisonous gas, which was hard to detect. Miners would carry a small bird, such as a canary, in a cage. If the bird became unconscious, they knew

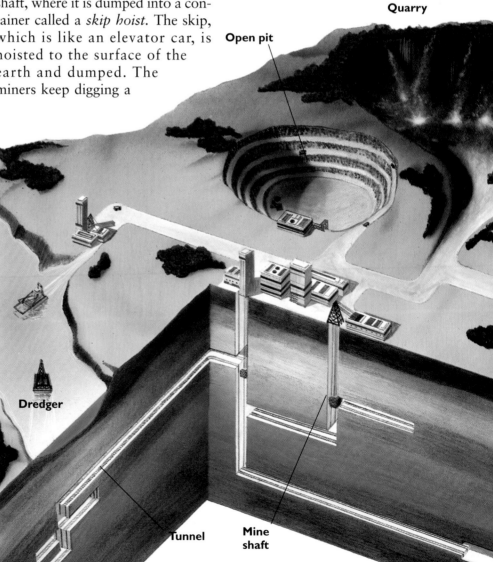

Quarry

Open pit

Dredger

Tunnel

Mine shaft

A gold mine. Deep holes are drilled into the mine walls in which explosives are placed to blow the rocks apart. Rubble is also taken from the rock face, crushed, and the gold separated out.

that the air was bad and that poisonous gas might be around. Without an early warning, the miners could have died from poisonous fumes. Today, groups such as the U.S. Bureau of Mines work to improve mine safety. One invention that saved many miners' lives was the safety lamp. Invented in 1815 by Sir Humphry Davy, it prevented the flame of the miner's lamp from setting off a gas explosion. Today, miners use electric lamps. Bad air and poisonous gas are detected by special devices and removed. Huge fans blow fresh air through the mine shafts. Safety teams are trained to rescue fellow miners in the event of an accident.

Conserving Minerals

In the first few thousand years of mining, little of the world's supply of minerals was used up. In the last 100 years, much more ore has been mined than in all the time before. Once ore is mined, it cannot be replaced. Some countries will have very little ore left by the year 2000. The United States has already used up most of its best ore. For example, all the richest iron ore is gone. Because of new ways of prospecting and better methods of mining the poorer kinds of ore, the United States still has a fairly large reserve of many minerals. As the population grows, the amount of reserve used up each year will increase. This

The "Big Hole" at Kimberley, South Africa, is an old diamond mine that was dug out last century by thousands of miners working with picks and shovels. They dug out more than 25 million tons of rock to make a hole 1,640 feet (500 m) across and nearly 1,300 feet (400 m) deep.

Some metals can be obtained from sands. Titanium used in alloys (steel) is extracted from some rich sands, such as those on the Australian coasts.

amount can be lessened by *recycling*—or reusing—metals. You can help by collecting used cans and other kinds of junk metal and selling them to junk dealers or recycling them yourself. The junk will be melted and used to make new metal products. This will make it unnecessary to take more ore from the earth to get the metal.

▶ ▶ ▶ ▶ **FIND OUT MORE** ◀ ◀ ◀ ◀
Coal; Gold; Gold Rush; Metal; Mineral; Quarrying

MINIATURE

Miniatures are paintings done in a very small size. The artist must use very thin, pointed brushes. The paintings are about the size of those shown here.

Miniature painting of the kind called an *illumination*—that is, an illustration for a book—was popular in Europe all through the Middle Ages, and in the Near East and India at various periods, beginning with the 1200s in Persia. Even after the beginning of book printing, miniaturists were hired to add illustrations. In Europe, small portraits the size of lockets were also called miniatures. These were popular from the 1500s until the invention of photography in the 1800s.

In a medieval calendar, each month had a miniature picture showing an important activity of that month. The *November* miniature (shown here) shows a swineherd with his dog taking care of the pigs. Two other persons are trying to fetch pigs that

▲ **A Persian miniature painted sometime during the 1600s. Before photography, miniature likenesses were convenient, as they could be carried around easily.**

▲ *November,* **a miniature filled with painstaking detail and color, painted by the Limbourg brothers in France during the early 1400s.**

have wandered into the woods. The trees are changing color, and in the background you can see a castle. Imagine the fine brushwork it took to paint such a tiny picture with so much detail!

▶ ▶ ▶ ▶ **FIND OUT MORE** ◀ ◀ ◀ ◀
Oriental Art; Painting

MINISTRY

SEE CLERGY

MINNESOTA

Minnesota is called "The Land of Ten Thousand Lakes," but the correct number is even larger. If you count all the lakes 25 acres (1 sq. km) or more in size, you will find more than 11,000 of them. The smaller lakes are far too numerous to count. Millions of years ago glaciers created these lakes.

The Land and Climate
Minnesota is in the north central part of the United States. Canada lies along its northern border. To the west are North and South Dakota. The state of Iowa lies to the south. Wisconsin and Lake Superior are on the eastern border.

LEARN BY DOING

You can create your own miniature using watercolors or colored pencils. Cut out a piece of white cardboard about three inches (8 cm) square. Draw in your picture with black pencil and then color it in. If you paint with watercolors, be sure to use a thin brush with a fine point. Mix very little water with the paints so that the colors do not run together in your painting. Keep the points of colored pencils sharp.

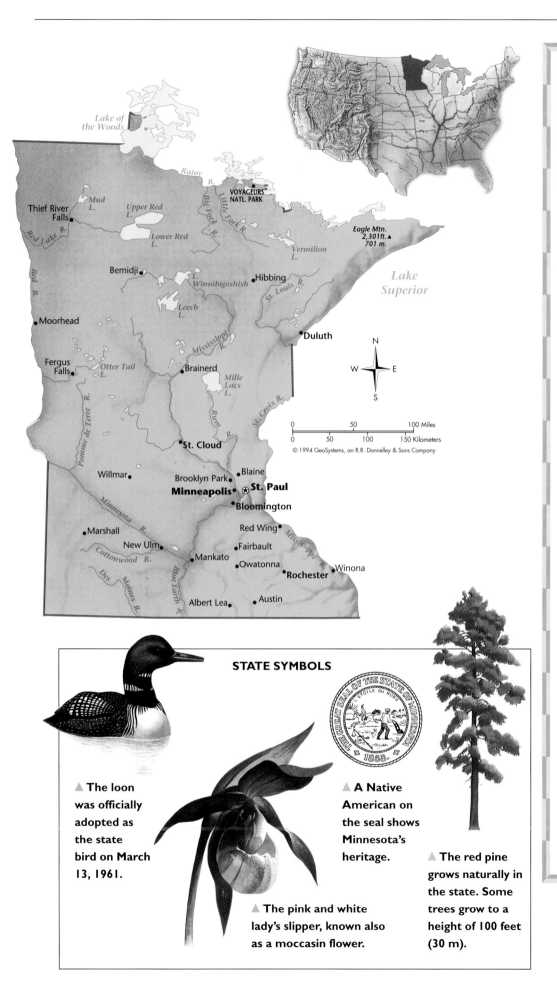

Lake of the Woods

Rainy

Thief River Falls

Mud L.

Upper Red L.

Lower Red L.

VOYAGEURS NATL. PARK

Big Fork R.

Little Fork R.

Eagle Mtn. 2,301ft.▲ 701 m.

Vermilion L.

Lake Superior

Bemidji

Hibbing

L. Winnibigoshish

St. Louis R.

Red Lake R.

Red R.

Moorhead

Leech L.

Fergus Falls

Otter Tail L.

Brainerd

Mississippi R.

Duluth

Mille Lacs L.

Pomme de Terre R.

St. Croix R.

Rum R.

St. Cloud

N
W   E
S

0   50   100 Miles
0   50   100   150 Kilometers
© 1994 GeoSystems, an R.R. Donnelley & Sons Company

Willmar

Blaine

Brooklyn Park

Minneapolis   ⊛ St. Paul

Bloomington

Minnesota R.

Marshall

New Ulm

Red Wing

Cottonwood R.

Mankato

Fairbault

Mississippi R.

Blue Earth R.

Des Moines R.

Owatonna

Rochester

Winona

Albert Lea   Austin

MINNESOTA

Capital
St. Paul
(277,235 people)

Area
84,068 square miles
(217,719 sq. km)
Rank: 12th

Population
4,375,099 people
Rank: 21st

Statehood
May 11, 1858
(32nd state admitted)

Principal river
Minnesota River

Highest point
Eagle Mountain:
2,301 feet (701 m)

Largest city
Minneapolis
(368,383 people)

Motto
L'Etoile du Nord
("The Star of the
North")

Song
"Hail Minnesota"

Famous people
Walter Mondale, F. Scott
Fitzgerald, Hubert
Humphrey, Charles
Schulz, Sinclair Lewis

STATE SYMBOLS

▲ The loon
was officially
adopted as
the state
bird on March
13, 1961.

▲ A Native
American on
the seal shows
Minnesota's
heritage.

▲ The red pine
grows naturally in
the state. Some
trees grow to a
height of 100 feet
(30 m).

▲ The pink and white
lady's slipper, known also
as a moccasin flower.

▲ Farmers came from the eastern states and throughout Europe to farm the fertile soils of Minnesota's plains. Minnesota is a leading producer of oats, corn, soybeans, and dairy products.

▲ Sailing on Lake Calhoun, one of Minnesota's many lakes, is enjoyed by local people and vacationers alike.

1712

Besides being a land of lakes, Minnesota also has many rivers and streams. The state is named after the Minnesota River. The word Minnesota means "sky blue water" and comes from the Sioux tribal language. Minnesota is also called the "North Star State" and "Gopher State."

Minnesota has two main parts. They are very, very different. Long ranges of hills run across the northeastern part of the state. This region was once heavily forested in white pine and Norwegian pine, but people have cut down many of the trees. Some people needed clear land for farming. Others cut the trees for lumber. Large areas of woodland remain, and along with the lakes, Minnesota's forest areas have become popular vacation lands. Southern Minnesota and the valley of the Red River in the northwest were once prairie grasslands. Few trees grew in these areas, except along the banks of rivers. The prairie has now disappeared, its fertile soil having been plowed, and it is now covered with rich farmlands.

Minnesota has cold winters and hot summers. The northern part of the state is extremely cold in winter. Rain and snow are much heavier in the east than in the west.

History
Sioux Native Americans once lived in the Minnesota forests. By the 1600s, the Ojibwa (Chippewa) Native American tribe had moved into northern Minnesota. The Ojibwas were members of a large eastern tribe. Europeans were taking over the tribe's hunting grounds in the east, so the Ojibwas were forced to move westward. They fought the Sioux for new hunting grounds.

Europeans first came to Minnesota at about the same time. A French explorer named Daniel Greysolon arrived in 1679. His title was Sieur Duluth (or Dulhut). The city Of Duluth, Minnesota, is named in his

▼ Minnesota is known also as the "Gopher State." In 1857, a cartoon pictured rogue railroad men as gophers. The animal is common in the central and western prairies and does much damage.

honor. Duluth made friends with the Sioux and claimed the whole region of Minnesota for the king of France. In 1680, Father Louis Hennepin, a French priest, discovered and named the Falls of St. Anthony. The city of Minneapolis now stands near the spot on the Mississippi River where the Falls of St. Anthony are located. No boats from the south could sail past the falls, which provided waterpower for the first settlements there.

French traders bought furs from the Native Americans, paying them with goods. The British first and the Americans later took over this profitable fur trade.

The U.S. Government had gained control of Minnesota by the early 1800s. In 1819, U.S. soldiers built Fort St. Anthony near the falls discovered by Father Hennepin. The soldiers built a flour mill and a sawmill to produce lumber. Both mills were run by waterpower from the falls. These were the first manufacturing plants in Minnesota.

The settlement that grew around the falls became the city of Minneapolis. A neighboring town, St. Paul, began as a Native American village. By 1840, most of the people living there were French hunters and traders. They built a log church and named it for St. Paul. Soon people began calling the entire town by that name. Minneapolis and St. Paul grew until their boundaries touched. Now the two cities are side by side and look like one large city. They are called the "Twin Cities."

In the 1850s, the governor of the Minnesota region persuaded the Sioux and Ojibwa tribes to give up large areas of land. Settlers flocked in, coming mostly from the northeastern states. Many Irish, Norwegian, Swedish, German, English, and Canadian people moved to Minnesota, which became a state in 1858. When the Civil War started, the new state provided a regiment of soldiers for the Union Army. The Sioux saw the war as a chance to regain their land. In 1862, Sioux warriors attacked the white settlements, but the Sioux were eventually defeated.

The state developed rapidly after the Civil War. Lumbering became the leading industry for a while. Wheat growing also became an important business. The wheat was taken to Minneapolis, where mills ground it into flour. Iron mining in northeastern Minnesota began in 1884. The iron ore was hauled to Duluth on the coast of Lake Superior. It was then carried eastward across the Great Lakes. In 1892, the first ore was discovered in the famous Mesabi Range. The ore was very near the surface of the ground, and huge quantities were mined. The range's best ore is now gone, but the lower-grade ore, called *taconite*, still is being mined. Minnesota remains the leading iron-mining state.

Working in Minnesota

Manufacturing is now the principal source of income in Minnesota. More than half of all Minnesota's factory workers are employed in or near the Twin Cities. Office equipment, computers, farm equipment, and mining machinery are important products. Food processing is also one of the state's major industries. Flour and butter are valuable food products. Lumbering is still one of the basic industries. The tall tales about the giant lumberjack Paul Bunyan and his Blue Ox, Babe, were told in

▲ **Many new skyscrapers grace the skyline of downtown Minneapolis.**

the lumber camps of Minnesota.

Agriculture is the second most important source of income in Minnesota. Cattle, hogs, and poultry are raised. Minnesota is known for its dairy products. Corn is the leading crop, but much of it is fed to livestock. Other crops, in their order of importance, include soybeans, hay, oats, and wheat.

Even before the Civil War, Southern planters often traveled up the Mississippi River to St. Paul for summer vacations. Today, recreation and tourism are a big business in Minnesota. Fisherman and hunters come from all over the country to the state's deep forests and plentiful lakes. During the summer, the lakes are full of boats, canoes, water-skiers, swimmers, and skin divers. In winter, cross-country skiing, ice hockey, ice skating, iceboating, snowmobiling, and ice fishing are popular sports.

▶ ▶ ▶ ▶ **FIND OUT MORE** ◀ ◀ ◀ ◀
Bunyan, Paul; Flour Making;
Fur and Fur Trading; Great Lakes;
Iron and Steel; Ojibwas; Prairie;
Sioux; Westward Movement

▲ **Minnesota's capital, St. Paul, annually holds a winter carnival, which has become a major tourist attraction. Pictured here is a gigantic ice sculpture at that event.**

A famous mirage called Fata Morgana occurs in the Strait of Messina, between Italy and Sicily. Unusual shapes found in rocks and cliffs appear as castle towers and walls.

MIRAGE

On a hot summer day, while driving along the highway, you may have noticed puddles of water on the highway in front of your car. But when the car got closer, the puddles of water disappeared. What you saw was a mirage.

Where do mirages come from? On a hot day, the heat soaks into the highway. The hot pavement then throws some of the heat back into the air, like a radiator inside a house. This hot air floats about a foot above the highway. The top of the layer of hot air acts like a mirror. The hot air reflects the light coming from the sky, just as a mirror does. The "water"

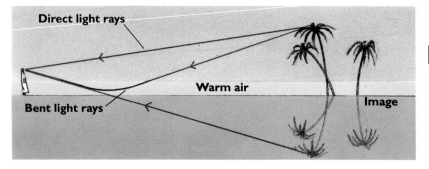

▲ A mirage is formed when rays of light are *refracted,* or bent, by a layer of warm air near the ground. This is why mirages are common in hot countries.

▼ Mirages often occur in desert places. Travelers see stretches of water that are not there at all.

that you see is the blue sky reflected on hot air floating on top of the highway. Depending on the highway color and the angle at which a person sees it, the "puddles of water" in the mirage can look dark or shiny.

Mirages can happen wherever there is a hot sun beating down on a flat surface. In the desert, the sand becomes very hot. The layer of hot air above the sand then reflects the

sky, and a traveler happily thinks he or she is looking at a cool oasis in the distance.

A second kind of mirage can occur, particularly over the sea and in polar regions, in which distant objects such as ships and icebergs seem to be floating in the air. Sometimes objects below the horizon can be seen in the sky. This occurs when the ground is colder than the air, so that the air close to the ground is colder than the air higher up. Where the cold air and warmer air meet, the warmer air acts like a mirror in the sky. Thus, a mirage is a kind of atmospheric optical illusion.

▶▶▶▶ **FIND OUT MORE** ◀◀◀◀
Light; Mirror

MIRROR

A mirror is any smooth surface that reflects light. Most mirrors in houses are made of glass. The glass is polished until it is very smooth. Then a film of silver or aluminum is laid on the back of the glass. The silver or aluminum backing reflects the light that falls on the glass. When you stand in front of a mirror, you see yourself because the light is reflected

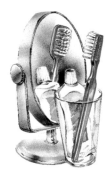

▲ Convex mirrors make things look smaller and give a wider view, useful for drivers.

◀ Concave mirrors make things look larger, useful in the bathroom.

from you to the mirror and back from the mirror into your eyes.

The ancient Egyptians had highly polished bronze mirrors. In 1835, a German scientist, Justus von Liebig, discovered how to put a film of silver on the back of a piece of glass.

Mirrors do not have to be straight. Curved mirrors are used to direct light rays. An automobile headlight, for example, has a curved back made of polished metal that acts like a mirror. The metal reflects the light so as to send a beam shining straight in front of the car. The driver can then see where he or she is going when driving at night. If you take off the front of a flashlight, you can see how

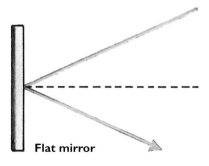

Flat mirror

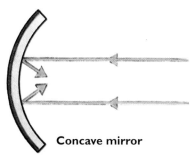

Concave mirror

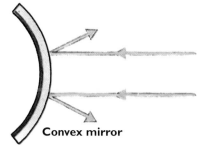

Convex mirror

▲ A flat mirror gives a true image. A concave mirror produces a magnified image. A convex mirror, which curves outward, gives a smaller, wider image.

the inside of the flashlight is curved the same way, to concentrate the light. Some telescopes are made of a large curved mirror. The mirror collects light rays that come from distant stars and directs all the rays to one place so they can be seen clearly.

▲ Curved mirrors can distort the light reaching our eyes so much that they give us a funny, distorted view of ourselves. Such mirrors are often found in fairgrounds.

▶▶▶▶ FIND OUT MORE ◀◀◀◀
Light; Mirage; Telescope

LEARN BY DOING

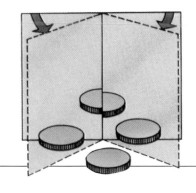

It is possible to see a reflection of a reflection. Lay a penny on a table. Hold two mirrors behind it with the edges touching. Now move the outer edges forward. How many pennies can you see?

▲ By A.D. 900, the Chinese had designed an arrow with an exploding gunpowder tube. This traveled a long distance.

▲ During World War II, the Germans built the V2 Rocket. It was 46 feet (14 m) high and carried 11,023 pounds (5,000 kg) of explosives.

▶ A radar system may track both the missile and its target. A computer reads the radar signals and controls the missile's guidance system to guide it to the target by radio.

☀ MISSILE

Any object thrown, fired, or projected in some way at a target can be called a missile. Bullets and spitballs are missiles. But the word is most frequently used to refer to a military weapon that is usually powered by a rocket engine. A missile may carry a *warhead,* consisting of explosives, used to destroy the missile's target.

A *guided missile* is guided all the way to its target either by radio, radar, or laser command from the Earth or by a device within the missile. A *ballistic missile* follows a path that is preset before launch. It is guided by its own navigation system during the "boost phase" while it goes up. After its rocket engine burns out, it returns to Earth in an unguided path called a *ballistic trajectory.* The path is calculated beforehand.

Missiles are classified according to their launching point and target. *Air-to-air missiles* (AAM) are launched from airplanes and are aimed at other planes or at other guided missiles. *Air-to-surface missiles* (ASM) are launched from airplanes and are aimed at targets on the Earth. *Surface-to-air missiles* (SAM) are launched from the Earth to targets in the air, such as planes or other missiles. *Surface-to-surface missiles*

(SSM) are fired from launches on the Earth at targets on the ground. *Underwater-to-surface missiles* (USM) are fired from submarines at surface targets.

A *guidance* system is the method used to steer a missile toward its target. A missile's guidance system gives instructions to sensitive and complicated machinery (the *control system)* that keeps the missile on course. Missiles controlled by a *command* guidance system receive radio instructions from stations on the ground or from another aircraft. For *preset* guidance systems, all instructions and adjustments for direction, speed, and altitude are put into an automatic pilot in the missile before the launch. Missiles operating on the *beam rider* system follow, or ride, a radar beam that is aimed at the target. In *homing* guidance systems, the missile contains sensitive machines that pick up and *home* (follow automatically) in on the target's radar beams, heat, or noise. *Inertial* guidance is used in

▲ Some guided missiles are light enough to be carried by infantrymen.

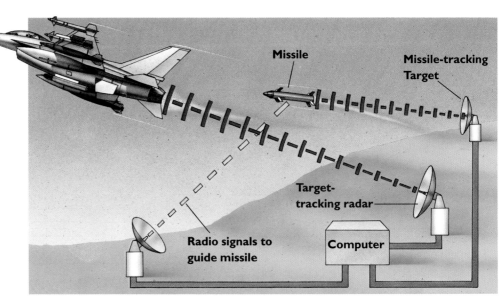

Missile

Missile-tracking Target

Target-tracking radar

Computer

Radio signals to guide missile

▲ The first jets were flown in the 1950s. Designers soon developed faster aircraft that carried more complex weapons. The F-16 is a lightweight fighter.

missiles with long *ranges* (traveling distances). Inertial guidance involves a system of gyroscopes and other equipment that pick up information during the flight about the missile's course, speed, and condition. This information is fed into the missile's computers, which provide directions.

Ballistic missiles, designed for nuclear attacks, come in three categories: *intercontinental ballistic missile* (ICBM), *intermediate-range ballistic missile* (IRBM), and *medium-range ballistic missile* (MRBM).

A guided missile can carry almost any kind of explosive charge, or warhead. Small anti-tank missiles may carry armor-piercing explosives. A large ICBM can carry many nuclear warheads, each programmed for a different target. They are known as MIRVs (multiple independently targetable re-entry vehicles).

The *propulsion* system of a missile may be a rocket engine, which carries its own oxygen, or an air-breathing engine, which depends on oxygen in the atmosphere. Since ballistic missiles often go outside the Earth's atmosphere, they are propelled by rocket engines. Rocket engines are capable of greater speeds than air-breathing engines. Some rocket engines use liquid fuel, which requires a complicated storage system. But modern rocket engines use solid fuel, which is easier and safer to store.

▶▶▶▶ **FIND OUT MORE** ◀◀◀◀
Gyroscope; Motion; Nuclear Energy; Orbit; Rocket; Space; Space Research; Submarine; Weapons

MISSIONARY

A missionary is a person who is dedicated to teaching and spreading a religious faith. Missionaries have been very important in the Christian religion. The first Christian missionaries were the 12 Apostles chosen by Jesus Christ.

The Roman Catholic Church was the first Christian body to organize its missionaries into *missions* (churches run by missionaries). Dominican and Benedictine monks led the earliest missions. The Jesuits and Franciscans later became large missionary groups. They started hundreds of colleges and established missions all over the world. Missionary work in the Protestant Church began around the 1700s.

Many early missionaries were killed by the people they were trying to help. Besides preaching religion, many missionaries have also been

▲ A warship firing short-range SAMs (surface-to-air missiles). The quantity of ballistic missiles have been cut back since the end of the Cold War in 1989.

▲ Missionaries from Europe had converted 150,000 Japanese to Christianity by the year 1580. This lessened the power of the Buddhists, whom the Japanese ruler Hideyoshi distrusted. But later he regarded Christianity as a dangerous threat to Japanese beliefs. In 1587, Christianity was banned.

▲ **The mission hospital that Albert Schweitzer set up at Lambarene, Gabon, Africa.**

teachers and doctors. Albert Schweitzer was a greatly admired "medical missionary" in Africa. Another famous missionary, John Eliot, came to America in the 1600s. He preached to the Native Americans in Massachusetts and translated the Bible into their language. California's greatest missionary was a Spanish Franciscan priest named Father Junípero Serra. He founded the first of his 21 California missions in 1769. He is buried in the beautiful mission of San Carlos Borromeo in Carmel, California.

▶▶▶▶ **FIND OUT MORE** ◀◀◀◀

Christianity; Salvation Army;
Schweitzer, Albert

> Mississippi has had several state capitals. Natchez was capital from 1798 to 1802, Washington from 1802 to 1817, Natchez again from 1817 to 1821, and Columbia from 1821 to 1822. Jackson has been the capital since then.

MISSISSIPPI

Have you ever heard of catfish farming? The state of Mississippi leads all other states in the raising of catfish. The homely catfish is tasty and provides a good source of protein. Many Mississippians and others like it. The catfish are reared in freshwater ponds until they are large enough to catch and sell. Most of Mississippi's catfish farms are in the region called "The Delta." People in other parts of the southern United States have taken up catfish farming, too.

The Land and Climate

Mississippi belongs to a region of the United States often known as the "Deep South." The state stretches northward from the Gulf of Mexico

to the state of Tennessee. The great Mississippi River forms the western boundary separating Mississippi from the states of Arkansas and Louisiana. The state of Alabama lies to the east.

The Delta lies in northwestern Mississippi. It is between the Mississippi River on the west end and the Yazoo and Tallahatchie rivers on the east. This region is flat and very fertile. For centuries, the Mississippi River spread over the land during spring floods. When the water drained off, *silt* (topsoil) that the river had been carrying was left on the land. Deep, rich soil was built up in this way. *Levees,* or embankments, were built in the 1800s to control the floods. The Delta then became the country's leading cotton region.

Traveling eastward from the Delta, you come to hilly country. The main ridge of hills, called the Bluff Hills, was once a rich and fertile area. But much of the soil has been worn out by the planting of cotton year after year. Plants cannot grow in this poor soil. This means that there are no plant roots to hold the soil together, so rain washes it away. After every rain, the gullies are a little deeper and wider.

As you near the eastern border of the state, you come to the Black Belt or Black Prairie—a region of rich soil and grassland. Many of the early settlers made their farms here, for there were no forests to clear away. Prairie farmers now raise dairy cattle and chickens, as well as crops.

In the northeast corner of Mississippi are the Tennessee Hills. Slopes are steep here. They are difficult to plow and plant, and most farms are very small. Crops not found in other parts of Mississippi are raised in the Tennessee Hills. Among these are apples, grapes, and tobacco.

The southernmost part of the state has two sections. One section covers most of the southeast. It is known as the Piney Woods or Pine Hills. Much

STATE SYMBOLS

◄ **The mockingbird is named for its habit of copying bird calls.**

► **The beautiful white magnolia chosen in 1952.**

◄ **The southern magnolia was chosen by Mississippi schoolchildren. It became the official state tree in 1938.**

◄ **The olive branch represents peace; the arrows, an ability to fight.**

THE GREAT SEAL OF THE STATE OF MISSISSIPPI

MISSISSIPPI

Capital and largest city
Jackson
(196,637 people)

Area
47,716 square miles
(123,575 sq. km)
Rank:32nd

Population
2,573,216 people
Rank: 31st

Statehood
December 10, 1817
(20th state admitted)

Principal rivers
Mississippi River
Pearl River

Highest point
Woodall Mountain;
806 feet (246 m) in the
northeastern corner of
the state

Motto
Virtute et Armis
("By Valor and Arms")

Song
"Go, Mississippi"

Famous people
William Faulkner, Elvis
Presley, Leontyne Price,
Eudora Welty

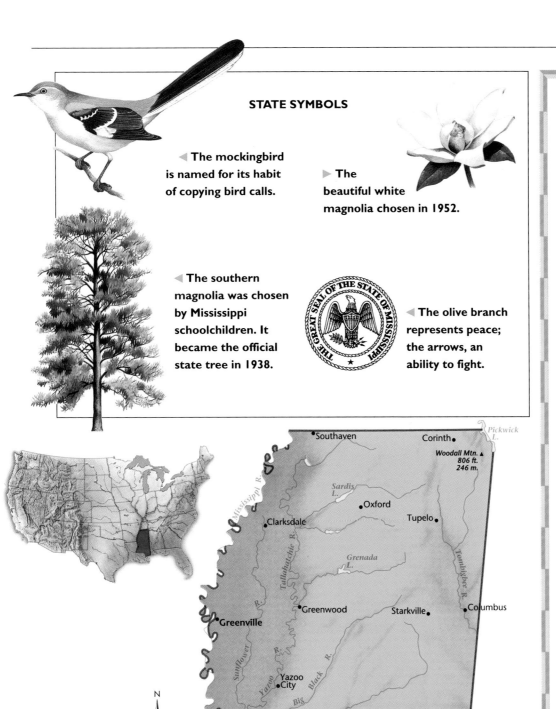

Southaven
Corinth
Pickwick L.
Woodall Mtn. ▲
806 ft.
246 m.
Sardis L.
Oxford
Tupelo
Clarksdale
Mississippi R.
Tallahatchie R.
Grenada L.
Tombigbee R.
Greenwood
Starkville
Columbus
Greenville
Sunflower R.
Yazoo R.
Black R.
Yazoo City
Big
Ross Barnett Res.
Vicksburg
⊛ Jackson
Meridian
Chickasawhay R.
Pearl R.
Leaf R.
Natchez
Laurel
Mississippi R.
Homochitto R.
Hattiesburg
McComb
Wolf R.
Pascagoula R.
Gulfport Biloxi Pascagoula
Mississippi Sound
GULF OF MEXICO

N
W   E
S

0   25   50   75 Miles
0   25   50   75   100 Kilometers

© 1994 GeoSystems, an R.R. Donnelley & Sons Company

▲ A New Orleans steamboat travels slowly along the Mississippi River. Today, steamboats carry mainly tourists, but back in the 1800s they provided a necessary service for passengers and goods.

New land is being created from silt at the mouth of the Mississippi River at the rate of a mile (1.6 km) every 17 years.

of the soil there is poor. The hardy pine trees are the only plants that grow well. In the past, a large amount of timber was wastefully cut. The soil was left bare, except for stumps. But many areas have now been replanted. The northwestern part of the Piney Woods has the best soil. It is too thin for cotton, but tomatoes and other vegetables grow well there.

South of the Piney Woods lies Mississippi's coast. It is a small part of the long Gulf Coastal Plain. Its sandy soil is not good for growing crops, and some of the land is marshy. But mild winters and the beauty of the blue Gulf of Mexico bring many tourists to the coast.

The town of Biloxi is a busy fishing port. The Biloxi fishing fleet brings in Gulf shrimp, oysters, and fish called menhaden. Much of the seafood is processed at canneries in the town. Other factories make fertilizer from the menhaden.

Winters in Mississippi are short, and there are few really cold spells. The hot, drowsy summers are typical of most of the Deep South. The best season is fall. Nights are cool then, and the days are sunny and pleasantly warm.

History

Three Native American tribes lived in the Mississippi region before the European settlers arrived. They were the Choctaw, the Chickasaw, and the Natchez. The tribes lived mainly by farming. Spaniards visited the region in the 1500s. But the first European settlements were founded by the French. The colonist Pierre le Moyne, whose title was Sieur d'Iberville, brought settlers to what is now Mississippi in 1699. His party built a fort and village on the Gulf coast. This settlement became the town of Ocean Springs.

Most of Mississippi was in the area that France lost to Great Britain in 1763, at the end of the French and Indian War. After the Revolutionary War, Mississippi came under the control of the United States. Americans from the East flocked to Mississippi, attracted by the fertile soil that was ideal for raising cotton. Planters bought land in the Delta and hill country of Mississippi. To help them work the land, they marched gangs of black slaves westward to the big plantations. In 1806, improved Mexican cotton was introduced.

Mississippi became a state of the Union in 1817. In 1861, it broke away from the Union and helped to form the Confederate States of America. Jefferson Davis, who became president of the Confederacy, was living in Mississippi at the time. The abolition of slavery at the end of the Civil War almost destroyed the state's only big business, cotton raising. The cotton plantations had depended entirely on their slave labor. The old way of life in the South began to break up.

These troubled times are vividly described in the novels of the great American writer William Faulkner. Faulkner was born in New Albany, Mississippi. The cotton business began to improve again after *sharecropping* was adopted. Under this system, the landowners rented land to people, mostly blacks, who worked the land and paid their rent with a share of the crop. The share-croppers made a very poor living.

Poverty is still Mississippi's worst problem. But the state is encouraging new industries, and many people now have a chance to earn more than their parents did. Another old problem has troubled Mississippi—discrimination against blacks, who make up more than one-third of the population. Civil rights leaders, such as Medgar Wiley Evers, have worked to alter these conditions. In 1963, Medgar Evers was shot and killed. But his brother, Charles Evers, was elected mayor of Fayette in 1969, becoming the first black mayor in Mississippi since 1875. He was reelected in 1973 and 1977. More blacks are now voting, and more blacks have been elected to public office in the 1980s and 1990s.

Working in Mississippi

Mississippi still looks like the home of country people. The land is mostly green fields and shady forests. However, almost half of the state's people live in urban areas, working in various industries. Lumber, wood products, clothing, transportation equipment, and processed foods are the main products. Factories bring the most wealth to the state, whose chief industrial center is Jackson, the capital. Oil and natural gas are found in southern Mississippi. The state has several large oil refineries.

Agriculture is still a major business. Cotton is no longer as important as it was in days gone by. But it is still the leading crop. Soybeans and rice are also valuable crops.

The raising of livestock—mostly cows and chickens—now brings in more money than all the crops put together.

Another important industry in Mississippi is tourism. Visitors come to the colorful state festivals, such as the Shrimp Festival at Biloxi. In March and April, they take part in the annual Natchez Pilgrimage. Some of the most elegant plantation houses were built around the town of Natchez before the Civil War, and these are still standing. People can visit these historic buildings, surrounded by the magnolia trees that have given Mississippi its nickname—the Magnolia State.

▶▶▶▶ **FIND OUT MORE** ◀◀◀◀
Choctaws; Civil Rights Movement; Civil War; Confederate States of America; Cotton; Davis, Jefferson; Gulf of Mexico; Mississippi River; Slavery

▲ **Pre–Civil War mansions that belonged to the cotton plantation owners are well preserved in Mississippi and attract many tourists.**

▼ **A drawing of a burial mound. From about 700 to the 1700s, Native American tribes in the Mississippi area built many mounds. Most of these were used for burying the dead. Earth, rocks, and other natural materials were piled up. The size of the mound increased as more bodies were added to it. Often gifts were included for use in the afterlife.**

The state ranks among the top ten as an oil producer. Oil and natural gas are drilled from many offshore wells in the Gulf of Mexico.

The Mississippi is one of the world's great rivers. Coal, sand, gravel, petroleum, and many other industrial products are shipped along the river by barge from the Great Lakes to the Gulf Coast.

MISSISSIPPI RIVER

If you have read *The Adventures of Huckleberry Finn* by Mark Twain, you will know about the excitement of taking a raft down the Mississippi River. Early settlers traveled down the long, wide, and lazy Mississippi on rafts.

The Mississippi is the longest river in the United States. It flows southward from the region of the Great Lakes to the Gulf of Mexico. From its source in the state of Minnesota to its mouth in the state of Mississippi, the river flows about 2,350 miles (3,782 km). The Missouri River flows into the Mississippi. The two rivers together stretch about 3,860 miles (5,922 km). Only the Amazon River system in South America and the Nile River system in North Africa are longer. The Mississippi system has 15,000 miles (24,000 km) of waterways that can be used by ships and barges. Boats travel up the Mississippi and several of its *tributaries* (branch rivers). The major rivers flowing into the Mississippi are the Minnesota, Des Moines, Illinois, Missouri, Ohio, Arkansas,

and Red (joined by the Ouachita). (See the map with the article on UNITED STATES.)

The Ojibwa (Chippewa) Native Americans named the river "Messipi," meaning "big river." The European settlers mispronounced the Native American word, and it became the name we know today. The first European to see the river was probably Hernando de Soto, a Spanish explorer. De Soto explored the lower river valley in 1541.

French explorers came to the region more than 100 years later. Jacques Marquette, Louis Joliet, Sieur de La Salle, and others explored more of the river. France held the territory until 1763, when it passed to Britain. Spain also had control of the region, which became part of the United States by treaty in 1798 and as a result of the Louisiana Purchase of 1803.

American settlers moved westward to farm these new lands. They shipped goods downstream to the port of New Orleans on the Gulf of Mexico. Flat boats and barges hauled upstream the manufactured goods and provisions that the settlers

▶ The Mississippi River ranges from one-half mile (800 m) to 1 mile (1.6 km) wide. In July 1993, weeks of steady rains caused the river to spill over the floodwalls and damage property and crops for hundreds of miles.

needed. Fishing became an important river industry.

The early 1800s was the time of the famous stern-wheel riverboats on the Mississippi. With a shower of sparks, one riverboat would race another for the title of "fastest boat on the river." Mark Twain worked for a while as a riverboat pilot. He wrote about his adventures in *Life on the Mississippi*. After the Civil War, most of the riverboat traffic on the Mississippi was replaced by the railroads.

Today, river tugs push barges on the Mississippi. Barges carry cargo more cheaply than railroads. The amount of goods shipped on the river is increasing. "Old Man River" is again a major transportation route.

The Mississippi in most places is between one-half mile and 1 mile wide. Its depth is often between 50 and 100 feet (15 and 30 m). The river discharges an enormous amount of water into the Gulf of Mexico. The force of the current also carries downstream tons of topsoil, sand, and gravel. Some of this *silt* is deposited on the riverbanks along the way. The rest has built up the big delta at the mouth of the river.

Spring rains and melting snow pour their waters into the Mississippi. For many years, the river flooded its banks in the spring. The floodwaters spread the rich silt over the land and built up the farmlands of the river valley. But the floods are dangerous. The worst floods occurred in 1927, 1937, and 1993. Homes and farms were ruined. Many people and animals drowned. The government built high banks, or *levees*, in the 1950s to stop the river from overflowing. But the levees did not hold in all places in 1993. Damage caused by the flood of 1993 was estimated at more than $8 billion. Iowa, Missouri, and Illinois were hardest hit.

▶▶▶▶ **FIND OUT MORE** ◀◀◀◀
De Soto, Hernando; Ojibwas; River; Ships and Shipping; Twain, Mark

MISSOURI

The state of Missouri is sometimes called the "Gateway to the West," because it once was regarded as the main starting point for pioneers moving westward across the United States. The state's largest city, St. Louis, has the same nickname today. A great arch, known as the Gateway Arch, rises from a green park in St. Louis. This arch is taller than the Washington Monument in the nation's capital. It is built of stainless steel and shines in the sunlight.

The Land and Climate

Missouri is in the Midwest of the United States. It is bounded by Arkansas on the south; Oklahoma, Kansas, and Nebraska on the west; and Iowa on the north. The mighty Mississippi River forms the eastern boundary, separating Missouri from the states of Illinois, Kentucky, and Tennessee.

Rivers provide Missouri with water transportation in all directions. The Missouri River forms part of the state's western boundary and then flows across the center of the state to join the Mississippi. The river port of St. Louis grew up near the point where they join. A little to the north, the Illinois River flows into the Mississippi. The Ohio River joins the Mississippi to the south.

Northern Missouri is a region of flat farmlands. This region is part of the wide plain that curves west and south around the Great Lakes. In the western part of central Missouri is an area of rolling prairie land called the Osage Plains. South of the Missouri River, the Ozark Plateau covers most of southern Missouri. The plateau is a region of forested hills, sparkling lakes, and fish-filled rivers. In the extreme southeast corner of the state is a narrow section called the "Boot Heel." The land here is low and flat. It is part of the floodplain of the Mississippi River.

▲ The Law Courts at St. Louis framed by the Gateway Arch, designed by the architect Eero Saarinen.

Silver Dollar City, near Branson, has been reconstructed as an 1880s mining town. Visitors can watch demonstrations of crafts, such as candle dipping and broom making.

MISSOURI

Capital
Jefferson City
(35,481 people)

Area
69,676 square miles
(180,447 sq. km)
Rank: 19th

Population
5,117,073 people
Rank: 15th

Statehood
August 10, 1821
(24th state admitted)

Principal rivers
Missouri River
Mississippi River

Highest point
Taum Sauk Mountain:
1,722 feet (525 m) in
eastern Ozark Plateau

Largest city
St. Louis
(435,146 people)

Motto
Salu Populi Suprema Lex
Esto ("Let the Welfare of
the People Be the
Supreme Law")

Song
"Missouri Waltz"

Famous people
Thomas Hart Benton,
George Washington
Carver, Walt Disney,
Samuel Langhorne
Clemens (Mark Twain),
Joseph Pulitzer, Harry S.
Truman

© 1994 GeoSystems, an R.R. Donnelley & Sons Company

STATE SYMBOLS

▲ The clusters of white "flowers" on the flowering dogwood are leaflike structures that grow around the flower.

▲ The moon on the shield represents the new state. The two bears stand for courage.

▲ The bluebird has a deep, rich blue coloring on its head and back.

▶ The white hawthorn's color stands for the state's pure ideals.

Missouri is generally cold in winter, and snowfall is fairly heavy in the northern regions. Summers are hot and humid. But some days of cool, dry weather bring relief from the heat. The growing season lasts half the year. Rain is plentiful, especially in the southeast.

History

The Native Americans who once lived in Missouri belonged to several tribes. Those who most impressed the settlers were the Osage. They were taller than most Europeans and very athletic. Two other important tribes were the Fox and the Sauk. Most of the Native Americans grew crops on the fertile plains and hunted the wild buffalo.

In 1673, Father Jacques Marquette and Louis Joliet, two French explorers, paddled down the Mississippi in canoes, stopping briefly at the mouth of the Missouri River before traveling on. Soon French trappers and fur traders from New France (French Canada) arrived in the Missouri region. Several French trading posts were set up along the rivers. Stories of gold and silver in the region attracted French prospectors. The French found lead in southeastern Missouri and began mining it. About 1735, they built a port on the Mississippi as a base for shipping out the lead. They named the port St. Genevieve. This town is the oldest in Missouri. The river port of St. Louis was founded in 1764. It was named for a favorite saint of France. The port was built as a fur center. Furs were brought down the Missouri River to St. Louis. They were packed there for shipment to Canada.

The United States, under President Thomas Jefferson, bought the huge Louisiana Territory from France in 1803. Missouri was a part of the territory. Thousands of American pioneers were already living in Missouri. Native Americans seldom attacked American settlers in Missouri. But

▲ Dillard Mill is typical of Missouri's countryside, where traditional industries still employ a small rural work force. Although more and more young people are moving to cities.

some of the tribes sided with the British in the War of 1812. After this war, settlers came in ever increasing numbers. Most were from Southern states. Some settlers brought black slaves with them. The Missouri Territory applied for permission to join the Union in 1818.

Many people in other parts of the nation disagreed with the idea of slavery. They claimed that if Missouri joined the Union, slavery should not be allowed in the new state. In 1821, the U.S. Congress agreed on the so-called Missouri Compromise. The compromise allowed Missouri to join the Union as a slave state, but ruled that slavery should not be permitted in other areas of the region that had been the Louisiana Territory.

Paddle-wheel steamboats were now traveling up and down Missouri's rivers. They brought thousands of people from the East. Many of these people did not stay in Missouri. From St. Louis they went up the Missouri River to Independence. From there, or at Westport (now a part of Kansas City), they set out on the long and dangerous journey along the Oregon Trail to the West Coast. Independence was also the start of the Sante Fe Trail, connecting Missouri with Santa Fe in the Southwest.

After 1850, Northerners began settling in Missouri. With them came immigrants from Europe—mostly

In 1971, a U.S. postage stamp was issued to honor Missouri's 150th anniversary of statehood. The picture on the stamp was part of a wall painting by the Missouri-born artist Thomas Hart Benton. This famous wall painting can be seen in the Harry S. Truman Library in Independence.

The Gateway Arch is the tallest monument in the world. The stainless-steel parabolic arch in St. Louis, Missouri, completed in 1966, attracts many visitors. The arch commemorates the westward expansion after the Louisiana Purchase of 1803.

As a memorial to Winston Churchill, former British prime minister, a church in London was taken down and rebuilt in 1965 at Westminster College in Fulton, Missouri. Churchill had made a famous speech there about the "iron curtain" of Communism.

Irish and Germans. The ideas of the new settlers often differed from those of the earlier settlers from the South. It was the beginning of conflict. When the Civil War broke out, Missourians fought Missourians. Some declared that the state was one of the Confederate States. Others declared that Missouri was loyal to the United States. This second group had strong Union forces on its side.

By the time the war ended, the old Missouri was no more. Covered-wagon days were over. The slaves had been freed. Blacks now raised cotton on rented lands. They were called *sharecroppers,* because their rent was a share of the crop. Steamboats had lost business to the new railroads. St. Louis had become one of the nation's leading rail centers. Kansas City, too, was growing, but it took more than a century to overtake St. Louis as the state's largest city. Agriculture, mining, and manufacturing were developing rapidly.

A great fair was held in St. Louis in 1904. It celebrated the Louisiana Purchase of 1803. In 1927, a group of St. Louis business executives gave a young American aviator, Charles Lindbergh, money to build an airplane. Lindbergh named his airplane *The Spirit of St. Louis.* He amazed the world by flying it to France on the first nonstop solo flight across the Atlantic Ocean.

Working in Missouri

St. Louis is the principal center of Missouri's major industry, manufacturing. The leading product of both state and city is transportation equipment. Automobiles, trucks, buses, railroad cars, and airplanes are built in the St. Louis and Kansas City areas. Processed food and chemicals are also other important products.

Agriculture is Missouri's second largest industry. The state has fertile soil and a long growing season. About one-third of Missouri farms raise livestock, such as cattle (for beef and milk), hogs, sheep, horses, and mules. For a time in the early part of this century, Missouri was the world's chief producer of mules for farm work. Today, the tasks once done by mules are done by tractors and other machines. Chickens and turkeys are also raised, and crops include soybeans, corn, hay, and grapes. Strawberries and other fruits are grown in the state. Another land use is forestry, and important hardwoods grown in Missouri include black walnut, oak, and hickory.

Missouri also has a busy tourist trade. The writer Mark Twain was raised in the town of Hannibal. His book *The Adventures of Tom Sawyer* tells of a boy's experiences in a town like Hannibal. George Washington Carver, a black teacher and scientist who worked to help Southern farmers, was another famous Missourian. John Joseph Pershing, the general who commanded American troops in France during World War I, and Harry S. Truman, President of the United States, were both born in Missouri. Every year, thousands of people visit the places connected with the lives of these Missourians.

▶▶▶▶ **FIND OUT MORE** ◀◀◀◀
Carver, George Washington; Civil War; Louisiana Purchase; Oregon Trail; Truman, Harry S.; Twain, Mark; Westward Movement

MODEL MAKING

Playing with dolls, running a toy car, building a toy town, running an electric train—in all these activities you use models. The toy car, the doll, the buildings, and the train are all models of larger, real objects.

Models are not always smaller. Sometimes they are the same size as the real object (such as a play telephone), and sometimes they are larger (such as a model of a tiny insect). There are two kinds of models. One kind is a copy of something that is already in existence. A model car, airplane, or house; a model of an animal or a skeleton; a model of the atoms that make up a molecule—any of these things are *reproductions*, or models, of things that already exist. The second type of model is made by designing something that does not exist now or has not existed in the past. A model of a car of the future or a model of a new kind of airplane are examples of this type of model.

Models are used for educational purposes. They give you experiences that you could not otherwise have. By using models, you can see what a city on the moon might look like in the year 2300, or you can discover what a Native American village of long ago was like.

Some people earn their living making models. The models they make may be *architectural* to show what buildings will look like before they are built. Some models are *industrial* to be used as test models, such as an airplane in a wind tunnel. Other industrial models show what a product will look like before it is manufactured in great quantities. *Educational* models are used in teaching. A model of the human heart can help students understand more about the human body. A model of a city can help planners and government officials understand its needs and help them plan the city's future.

Models are often constructed dur-

LEARN BY DOING

To make a model room, find a cardboard box. Remove the lid, and place the box on its side. Cut out windows or draw them on the walls. Paint the walls, ceiling, and floor. You can make furniture using glue and various kinds of materials. Scraps of cloth can make rugs, curtains, etc.

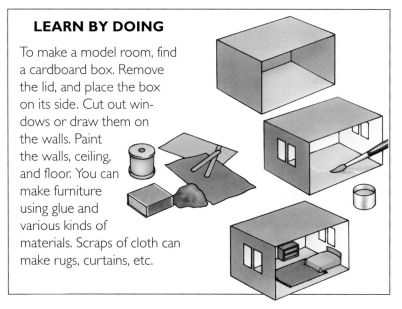

ing the making of a movie, when it would be very expensive to film the real thing, such as a battleship in a storm at sea. A professional model maker uses many kinds of materials, but good models can be made with ordinary, inexpensive materials. Cardboard tubes, paper, strong glue, balsa wood, wire, and modeling clay are good basic materials. You can also buy model-making kits for spaceships, airplanes, automobiles, and ships. These kits provide all the materials and instructions that you will need.

▶ ▶ ▶ ▶ **FIND OUT MORE** ◀ ◀ ◀ ◀
Carving; Clay Modeling;
Paper Sculpture

▼ **A model of one of the world's most famous buildings, the Taj Mahal in India. It enables people to see the whole building on a smaller scale and without having to visit India to see it!**

▲ The *Women of Avignon,* by Pablo Picasso. As a leading artist of the 1900s, Picasso challenged people's ideas.

▼ Vassily Kandinsky abandoned law to study painting. As in *Composition Number Four,* below, he felt that subjective matter could be dropped to increase impact of color and form.

🎭 MODERN ART

Every age in history has had its modern artists. They have most often been young people with new ideas which were different from those their masters were teaching. "Modern art," as we define it today, is a particular kind of art. Modern art is sometimes not *representational*—it doesn't have to look like anything. It may be just a pleasant blend of colors representing nothing more than the way the artist feels. Some *contemporary* (of our time) artists are *not* modern in their work—artists such as Andrew Wyeth. But very many contemporary artists work in modern art.

Modern art began in the second half of the 1800s, after the camera was invented. Photographs pictured things exactly as they were. So some artists saw no reason to do the same thing. Artists no longer had to paint portraits of children so their families would remember how they looked when they were little. A camera was better than an artist for that.

The French painter Paul Cézanne made the first great breakthrough to modern art. He worked slowly and carefully. He studied color and composition. He even destroyed many of his works before finally reaching a new kind of art. He felt that the shapes in a painting counted most.

He thought that all objects were one of three shapes—cylinder, sphere, or cone. A human body is a cylinder, a head a sphere. Three people together can form a cone shape. He changed the shapes of objects he painted, if he thought it would make a better picture. Cézanne used color to show perspective and three dimensions in a picture. His colors were bright, and he let the brush strokes show in his finished pictures. Cézanne was the pathfinder who led other artists to freer thinking in art.

Painting at about the same time as Cézanne was a Dutchman named Vincent van Gogh. He used paints strewn with grains of pigment that gave a lively look to the surface of his pictures. He used bright, new color combinations that showed his strong feelings. Sometimes he got so emotional when painting that he pressed paints right out of the tubes onto the canvas without blending them. Van Gogh paved the way for a form of art that became known as *expressionism,* in which modern artists painted to express feelings.

One of the great modern artists, Paul Gauguin lived and painted for a while with van Gogh. Gauguin then went to the South Pacific to paint. The beautiful, golden-colored people and the lush, tropical plants suited his kind of art. Gauguin would *abstract*—he would paint only those parts of a scene that he wanted. Scenes became patterns.

Another painter who loved color was Henri Matisse. His use of bright colors gave him and his followers the name of *Les Fauves*—The Wild Animals. Matisse was the leader of *Les Fauves.* Bright colors, strong lines and patterns, and a kind of joy in painting were his gift to art.

At about the same time as Matisse, another artist was developing in Paris—Pablo Picasso, probably the best-known modern artist. He and Georges Braque developed *cubism,* in which the artist tries to show all the sides of an object. Picasso created the huge canvas *The Women of Avignon* shown on page 1728. Looking at the picture at first is a bit of a shock. Picasso has sharpened the shapes of the women on the left. The two on the right have faces that are pulled out of shape. Besides the exaggerated features, you can see that the figures are made up of wedges or angular pieces, forming the many surfaces of cubism. The whole picture is fitted together tightly. Picasso moved on to other styles, but cubism as a style, remained popular.

After cubism arrived, breaking a painting into three-dimensional-looking chunks, it was only a small step to *nonobjective painting*, which does not even try to look like real objects. One of the leading nonobjective artists was Vassily Kandinsky of Russia. Kandinsky felt that art should come from the inner self—no model to look at, no landscape to see when painting. His pictures have titles such as *Red Spot* and *Composition Number Four*, which is shown on the opposite page. Bright color, irregular lines, and surprising curves fill his paintings.

Abstract expressionism became popular in the 1950s. A well-known abstract expressionist was Mark Rothko, whose painting *Composition* is shown at right. Abstract expressionism was called "action painting," because the artists put their whole selves into it. Jackson Pollock, a well-known U.S. artist, worked in this way on *Cathedral*.

Pop art became popular in the 1960s. Artists copied advertising art, such as the label of a tomato soup can. Critics constantly disagree on what is "good" modern art. The new trends in painting need the test of

▲ *Composition,* by the Latvian artist Mark Rothko.

▼ **Abstract expressionism introduced a completely different way of working for the artist. Some artists sprayed or poured paint directly on the canvas, which was usually placed flat on the floor. The traditional easel had to be abandoned.**

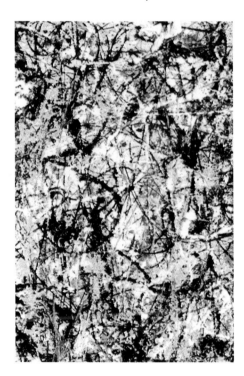

▲ **Detail from *Cathedral* (1947), painted by American abstract artist Jackson Pollock, who used enamel and aluminum paint on canvas. This thicket of lines is very busy to look at. Pollock painted with his canvas on the floor, so he could "literally be in the painting," as he explained in an interview.**

years before it becomes clear whether the art is "good" or if it will go out of style and be forgotten.

▶ ▶ ▶ ▶ **FIND OUT MORE** ◀ ◀ ◀ ◀
Abstract Art; Cézanne, Paul; Expressionism; Gauguin, Paul; Impressionism; Matisse, Henri; Picasso, Pablo; Surrealism; Van Gogh, Vincent

▲ The Mojave Desert receives less than 5 inches (13 cm) of rain a year.

Millions of years ago the Mojave Desert was covered by the Pacific Ocean. Then the coastal mountains were pushed up, cutting off the Mojave from the sea.

▼ Tourists admire the varied and ever-changing patterns of the beautiful sand dunes found in parts of the Mojave Desert.

MODERN DANCE

SEE DANCE

MOJAVE DESERT

The Mojave, or Mohave, Desert lies in southern California near Los Angeles. Along with the adjoining Colorado Desert, this wasteland covers about 20,000 square miles (50,000 sq. km), four times the size of the state of Connecticut.

The winds that blow eastward off the Pacific lose almost all of their moisture as they pass over the Coastal Range and the Sierra Nevada mountains. They have little moisture left to drop on the Mojave's dry sands. Any moisture is sucked up by intense desert heat. The record-high temperature in the United States was recorded in Death Valley, part of the Mojave, on July 10, 1913. It was 134 degrees Fahrenheit (56.6°C) *in the shade!*

The desert terrain consists of desert basins, low mountain ranges, outcroppings of lava, and cinder cones of extinct volcanoes. A few desert-type plants and animals still manage to live in the extreme conditions. Cactus plants store water in their thick stems. Grasshopper mice feed on scorpions and other small prey.

Some intermittent streams are present in the valleys of the desert. The largest, the Mojave River, flows mainly underground. In Antelope Valley in the western part, farmers draw up underground water to irrigate crops, such as alfalfa. Well water from the Mojave is piped to surrounding resort areas, such as Palm Springs and Desert Hot Springs.

In the 1890s, prospectors looking for gold and silver came to the Mojave Desert. Only a few struck it rich. Today, valuable deposits of *boron* (a mineral used in jet and rocket fuels) and sodium sulfate are found there. Miners also drill for tungsten and other space-age metals.

▶▶▶▶ **FIND OUT MORE** ◀◀◀◀
California; Desert

MOLD

SEE FUNGUS

# MOLDOVA

Moldova is a small country in Eastern Europe. Until 1991, it was part of the former Soviet Union and was called Moldavia. Moldova is a land of broad river plains and rolling hills. It is bordered by Ukraine on the north, east, and south and by Romania on the west.

Two great rivers pass through Moldova on their way to the Black Sea. The Dniester (Dnestr) cuts across northern Moldova, and the Danube—Europe's longest river—touches Moldova's southern border with Ukraine and Romania. Another river, the Prut, forms most of Moldova's western border with Romania. The rivers provide important trading routes and the fertile valleys surrounding them provide good farming land.

Agriculture is Moldova's most important industry. Wheat and barley grow in the great river basins. A mild climate is well suited to grapes, which grow in the rolling hills of the western part of the country.

Moldova's culture and language

are closely linked to Romania. Throughout its turbulent history Moldova has looked to Romania for assistance and, at times, leadership.

The region now known as Moldova has been disputed for centuries. Control of its fertile farmlands ensured a rich supply of crops. In the 1600s and 1700s it was called Bessarabia. Russian Tartars and Turks of the Ottoman Empire struggled for control of the area, although the population was mainly of Romanian or Ukrainian origin.

Russia gained control in 1812, but in 1918, the region voted to become a province of Romania. The Soviet Union gained control in 1940, proclaiming it the Moldavian Soviet Socialist Republic. It became Roman-

ian again briefly during World War II, but Soviet control resumed in 1944.

Moldova discarded its Soviet name and declared independence in August 1991. Full independence followed in December. Since then there has been tension between Romanian-speakers, the majority, and Russians and Ukrainians who settled there during the Soviet era.

▶ ▶ ▶ ▶ **FIND OUT MORE** ◀ ◀ ◀ ◀
Romania; Russia; Russian History

MOLDOVA

Capital city
Chisinau
(506,000 people)

Area
13,127 square miles
(34,000 sq. km)

Population
4,341,000 people

Government
Republic

Natural resources
Minerals, including
lignite and gypsum

Export products
Wine, grapes, textiles,
food products

Unit of currency
Ruble

Official languages
Romanian, Ukrainian

▼ **A village in Moldova, dominated by its church. Most people in Moldova are members of the Eastern Orthodox Church. There was no religious freedom in Moldova until the break up of the Soviet Union.**

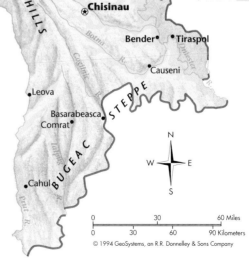

© 1994 GeoSystems, an R.R. Donnelley & Sons Company

▲ Deoxyribonucleic acid (DNA) is made up of two long strands coiled around each other into a double helix. This is the molecule that makes up the genes and chromosomes found in all living things.

▼ Moles are common in eastern parts of North America. The star-nosed mole has a circle of tentacles on its nose to help it find food.

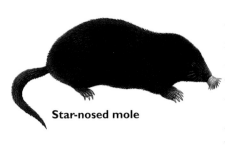

Star-nosed mole

Eastern mole

MOLECULAR BIOLOGY

Molecular biology is one of the youngest of the sciences. It studies the activity of cells by observing the behavior of the *molecules* that make up those cells. This study provides clues to the "building blocks of life." Their behavior can sometimes be predicted if a scientist is aware of their normal chemical reactions. Molecular biology uses the latest techniques to separate and analyze molecules. It is sometimes called "new biology."

Up to the early 1900s, the study of biology was separate from that of chemistry and physics. Then advances in all three fields led scientists to use the tools and methods of the other sciences.

The American mathematician Warren Weaver first used the term "molecular biology" in 1938 to describe such cooperation. He saw a "borderline area" where the three sciences could merge.

One of the most important aspects of molecular biology has been the work in *genes* and the way genetic information is stored and passed on in molecules. Whether you grow to be tall, or whether a plant blossoms white or pink, is defined by a code that can be studied using molecular biology.

Chemicals such as amino acids and carbohydrates make up the "building blocks" of living cells. In turn, much larger molecules (*macromolecules*) such as proteins govern more complicated cell functions. The chemical codes used by DNA, the macromolecule governing genetic behavior, were discovered in 1952 by two molecular biologists, James D. Watson of the United States and Francis H. C. Crick of Great Britain.

Their discovery led to some of the most fruitful discoveries in molecular biology or any science. Some advances in genetics have opened up the possibility of *genetic*

▲ Francis Crick (1916–) and James Watson (1928–). In 1953, they discovered the structure of DNA, the substance that transmits genetic information from one generation to the next. Crick (left) and Watson won a Nobel prize for their work, which altered the thinking on genetics.

engineering, where certain traits of a plant or human being can be helped chemically. This prospect scares some people, but few can argue with research that could isolate and replace genes that cause particular diseases such as cancer.

▶▶▶ **FIND OUT MORE** ◀◀◀
Biology; Cell; Chemistry; Genetics

MOLECULE

SEE CHEMISTRY

MOLES AND SHREWS

These animals are *insectivores*, which means "insect eaters." All insectivores look somewhat alike. Most have small, furry bodies and long, pointed noses. Their feet have tough, sharp claws that allow them to dig quickly through the ground. As the word insectivores tells you, they all eat insects, but they may also eat worms and other small, crawling animals. Moles and shrews are useful to farmers and gardeners because they get rid of many pests.

Moles are about 6 inches (15 cm)

► The mole spends nearly all of its time tunneling through the soil with its huge spadelike front legs. As sight is not important underground, its eyesight is poor.

long. They have thick fur on their bodies, but their pink tails have no fur. A mole's powerful front legs and claws turn outward, enabling it to tunnel rapidly through the earth. A mole can dig as much as 50 yards (45 m, or half the length of a football field!) underground in an hour. Moles dig almost constantly because they are looking for worms and insects to eat. If a mole could not find food for even 10 or 11 hours, it would die of starvation. Moles are almost blind because they spend all of their lives in their underground burrows and tunnels. Moles live in underground nests and tunnel away from the nests in search of food. They get rid of earth dug from their tunnels by pushing it upward. This forms the molehills that we often see in yards.

A shrew is a furry creature about the size of a small mouse. It looks like a mouse, except for its pointed snout. One kind of shrew, the white-toothed *pygmy shrew,* is the smallest nonflying mammal in the world. It is only about 2 inches (5 cm) long and weighs about as much as a cent.

Shrews are very active animals. A shrew has an enormous appetite, considering its size. A shrew eats three or four times its own weight in insects, worms, and mice every day.

The shrew, like the mole, must eat almost constantly to live.

A shrew is a very nervous animal. It will sometimes die of fright if it hears a loud, sudden noise. But the shrew will fight other larger animals. Like the mole, the shrew lives alone. Shrews have a disagreeable odor that prevents many of their enemies from bothering them. Some shrews have a poisonous bite.

▼ Moles make complicated underground tunnel systems that include sleeping and nesting chambers. Some chambers are also used for storing food. Excavated soil goes above ground as the familiar *molehills.*

Masked shrew

Short-tailed shrew

▲ The masked shrew is found across northern North America. The short-tailed shrew poisons its prey with its saliva.

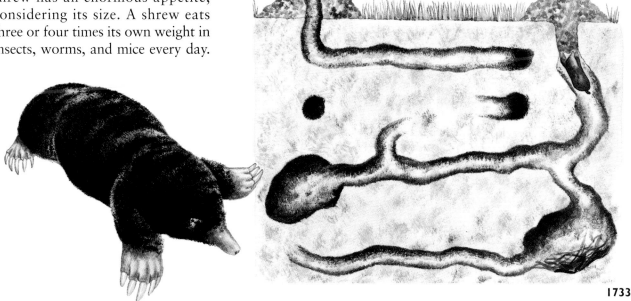

Hedgehog

▲ Hedgehogs are covered with sharp pointed quills. Their quills are set close together, making a protective covering against predators.

The white-toothed pygmy shrew is not only the smallest mammal in the world. It also has the shortest life span. Most shrews die before they are one year old.

Shrews live mostly in yards and woody areas. But people rarely see them, because they come out only at night and spend almost all their time hidden under leaves and bushes, eating and eating.

Hedgehogs are larger than most insectivores and live in Europe. They are about 10 inches (25 cm) long. Instead of fur, the hedgehog has tiny quills like the quills of a porcupine. When a hedgehog is attacked by another animal, it rolls itself up into a ball with its quills sticking out everywhere. But if a fox finds a rolled-up hedgehog, the fox will push the hedgehog into water. The hedgehog must then unroll to swim. As it swims, the fox can catch it.

The hedgehog makes its home under hedges and bushes. It comes out at night to feed on beetles, snails, worms, frogs, mice, and even poisonous snakes. The hedgehog has a high level of immunity to snake poison. When winter comes, the hedgehog builds a warm nest of leaves in its underground burrow. Then the hedgehog goes to sleep until spring comes again.

▶ ▶ ▶ ▶ **FIND OUT MORE** ◀ ◀ ◀ ◀
Mammal

MOLLUSK

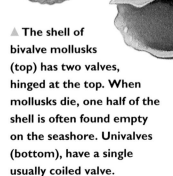

▲ The shell of bivalve mollusks (top) has two valves, hinged at the top. When mollusks die, one half of the shell is often found empty on the seashore. Univalves (bottom), have a single usually coiled valve.

The most familiar mollusks are probably the popular seafoods, such as clams and oysters. But there are more than 40,000 kinds of mollusks. They vary in size and shape— from tiny sluglike animals that could fit on the head of a pin to the giant squid.

Mollusks live on land, in salt water, and in fresh water throughout the temperate and tropical regions of the world. Certain snails live in the tops of tropical trees. But most mollusks live in the deep oceans.

Common Features of Mollusks

All mollusks are related, or alike, in certain ways. The word *mollusk* comes from a Latin word meaning "soft." Mollusks are *invertebrates*, having no bones at all. Their bodies are soft and somewhat shapeless. They have no joints or outer body parts, as do most other animals.

SHELL. Most mollusks have a hard shell that protects their soft bodies. Most of the shell is made of calcium carbonate. The inner surface of the shell of some mollusks is an iridescent, pearly layer. The shapes of mollusk shells vary greatly, but certain similar characteristics within each group serve as the basis for classification and identification.

Although a hard outer shell is typical of mollusks, some mollusks, such as slugs and squids, have shells inside the body, which are often very small. Octopuses have no shell.

INTERNAL ANATOMY. A mollusk's soft body is surrounded by an enveloping layer of tissue, called a *mantle*. Glands in the mantle produce the substances that harden to form the shell. In some mollusks, the mantle also performs other functions. The mantle of a clam has tube-shaped folds, called siphons, that help the clam eat and breathe.

Mollusks can stretch their bodies in and out of their shells by using strong muscles. The major means of movement is a muscular "foot." The size and shape of the foot is different in each group of mollusks, enabling it to be used for creeping, digging, or swimming.

Marine mollusks breathe through gills. Blood vessels, containing red, yellow, and colorless blood, carry oxygen-filled blood to the heart. Land mollusks also have gills, but they serve no purpose. Land mollusks breathe through pulmonary sacs formed from the mantle, which are similar to the sacs in lungs.

Most mollusks have a mouth, short gullet, fairly large stomach, and a long intestine. Inside the mouth is the *radula,* an organ like a file, which is used for scraping food off rocks or boring through hard substances. (A mollusk might bore a hole into sand or through the shell of another mollusk.) The stomach is connected to a digestive gland, in which food is absorbed into the blood. The mollusk's nervous system consists of nerve cords connected to masses of nerve cells, called *ganglia.*

REPRODUCTION. All mollusks hatch from eggs. In some mollusks, the eggs are fertilized while still inside the mother's body. Then they are laid in the sand under the water until they are ready to hatch. But in most mollusks, the eggs are released and then covered by sperm. Most of the eggs hatch as larvae, or immature animals very unlike their parents in appearance. Other mollusks, such as octopuses, look like tiny adults when they hatch.

How Mollusks Are Classified

Mollusks are divided into six classes. The most primitive class, Monoplacophora, contains the "living fossil" *Neopilina,* which looks a bit like a limpet. The class Amphineura includes the chitons, whose shells consist of eight overlapping plates. Members of the class Scaphopoda have open-ended shells resembling an elephant's tusks. All of these mollusks live in the sea, either at great depths or along the seashore.

GASTROPODS. Snails, abalones, and conchs belong to the class called Gastropoda. These are *univalve* (one-shelled) mollusks, with spiral-shaped shells. At the end of a gastropod's foot is a hard "door." When the foot is drawn into the body, the door fits snugly into the shell's opening. Many gastropods are able to seal themselves inside their shells. Some gas-

tropods attach themselves to rocks.

PELECYPODS. Mollusks of the class Pelecypoda are *bivalves.* Their shells have two parts that open and close like a book. Each shell section is called a *valve.* The valves are joined by a muscle that acts like a hinge. The muscle pulls the two valves shut when the ani-

◀ **The common cuttlefish has two extra long arms, useful to catch its prey. Its cuttlebone is often washed up on the beach.**

mal wants protection. When the valves are open, the soft mantle can be seen. Bivalve mollusks include clams, oysters, scallops, and mussels. Bivalve mollusks do not have heads. They use their wedge-shaped feet to move around and dig into mud.

CEPHALOPODS. These mollusks have reached a high state of development. Like other mollusks, they have soft bodies and mantles. But they do not look like other mollusks, and they have very different habits. The shells of squids, octopuses, and cuttlefish are inside their bodies. These mollusks have numerous *tentacles,* or arms, which help them move or hold their prey. Octopuses, squids, and cuttlefish are able to protect

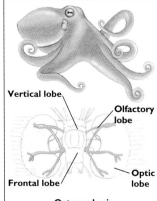

Vertical lobe

Olfactory lobe

Frontal lobe

Optic lobe

Octopus brain

In the animal world there are various designs of brains. The brain of the octopus is large and complex. It has 15 pairs of lobes and an extra nerve ring to help control the muscles of its lengthy eight arms.

▼ **When the limpet is out of the water at low tide, it uses its strong muscles to pull the shell tightly against the rock. Only a knife can pry it loose.**

Mollusks are little more than efficient sieves. They continually draw in a large amount of water and pump it over their gills to get food and oxygen. The Pacific oyster can take in as much as 6 gallons (24 liters) of water an hour.

▲ A pearl oyster opened to reveal the pearls inside. The oyster builds pearls by coating small foreign bodies, such as particles of sand, with layers of the substance *nacre*.

▲ The common garden snail oozes a trail of thick slime from the "foot," the lowest part of the body. The slime, or mucus, helps it to grip smooth surfaces such as glossy leaves and glass.

1736

themselves by shooting an inky fluid into the water to hide themselves. The *chambered nautilus* has an outer shell that is divided into chambers. As a new chamber grows, the nautilus moves into it, closes off the old one, and carries the entire shell along as it moves.

Giant squids are the largest mollusks, sometimes growing to 55 feet (17 m) long. They are swift swimmers, propelling themselves by ejecting streams of water, just as a jet plane is propelled by the streams of hot gas from its engines.

Valuable and Destructive Mollusks

Many kinds of bivalve mollusks are popular as seafood—especially oysters, clams, and scallops. But at least one bivalve is a destructive enemy of people. Shipworms are small bivalves that grow sharp-edged shells. They use these shells to tunnel through wood beneath the water, such as ship hulls and dock pilings, where they remain for the rest of their lives. As the body of the shipworm grows, the shell bores deeper into the wood often causing dangerous and costly damage.

Some bivalves, such as the pearl oyster and freshwater mussel, occasionally produce pearls used as jewels. Some bivalve shells are also sources of mother-of-pearl. Mollusk shells that have unusual or beautiful shapes are used as ornaments.

In some countries, octopuses and snails are considered to be great delicacies to eat. Snails are often kept in aquariums to eat any waste and to keep water clean. But some land snails and slugs are common garden and greenhouse pests.

▶▶▶▶ **FIND OUT MORE** ◀◀◀◀
Animal Kingdom; Clams and Oysters; Egg; Hobby; Marine Life; Octopus and Squid; Pearl; Shell; Snails and Slugs; Zoology

MOLTING

Insects, crustaceans, and certain other invertebrate animals, as well as reptiles, amphibians, birds, and many mammals, go through a process called *molting*. They shed their hair, feathers, shell, or skin.

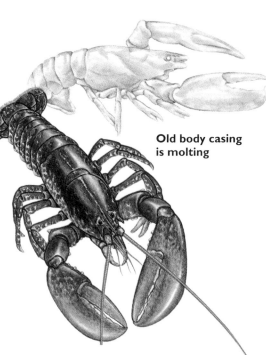

Old body casing is molting

▲ The lobster has a hard body casing. This is molted to reveal a new one beneath that expands and hardens.

When one covering is shed, a new one is grown. Molting is controlled by *hormones*, the chemical messengers of the body. *Ecdysone* is the molting hormone of insects.

Insect larvae have a hard outer skin, called a *cuticle*. The cuticle cannot grow or stretch. As the larva grows, it must shed its old cuticle and grow a new one that will fit. Insect larvae may molt as many as 20 times while they are developing. Molting is part of the insect development called *metamorphosis*.

The hard covering of a crustacean, such as a crab, is called a *shell*. When crustaceans molt, the new shell underneath the discarded shell is soft. Before the new shell hardens, the crustacean takes quantities of water into its body to make it swell. The soft shell expands and hardens over an extra-large body. When the water is released the body becomes smaller and there is room to grow.

Snakes, lizards, and amphibians molt by shedding their dead outer skin. The coloring of the skin becomes dull a few days before molting, and the covering of the eye turns cloudy. The animal stretches its skin by swelling some veins near the surface of its head. The skin splits, and the animal crawls out. You can sometimes find the skins left by snakes that have molted. Amphibians usually swallow the skin they have shed.

The word "molting" is also used to describe the shedding of feathers and hair by birds and mammals. This usually happens twice a year—in spring and in fall. Birds drop off their old feathers and grow new ones. Sometimes this changes the color of the feathers, which is important in mating and for hiding from enemies. Mammals shed hair in the spring. This makes their coat lighter during summer. In winter, they grow a thicker coat.

▶▶▶▶ **FIND OUT MORE** ◀◀◀◀

Amphibian; Bird; Crustacean; Feather; Fur; Hair; Hormone; Insect; Lizard; Mammal; Metamorphosis; Reptile; Shell; Skin; Snake

MONACO

The principality of Monaco lies on the French coast called the Riviera. It is squeezed between steep mountains and the Mediterranean Sea. Monaco is called a principality because it is ruled by a prince. Under a treaty signed with France in 1918, if there are no male heirs, the principality will automatically come under French rule. The tiny country has an area of less than one square mile (1.9 sq. km).

The capital is Monaco-Ville (Monaco-City). It is built on top of a cliff overlooking the sea. Prince Rainier III lives in the old fortresslike palace of Monaco-Ville. His beautiful wife, Princess Grace, who died in 1982, was the American motion picture star Grace Kelly before her marriage. Palace guards stand watch in candy-striped guardhouses, and the whole city has a charming medieval look.

Below the city lies the port of La Condamine. Its small harbor is usually crowded with luxurious yachts. Near the port is the world-famous Oceanographic Museum, with exhibits produced by research and exploration in the oceans and seas of the world. The well-known undersea explorer Jacques-Yves Cousteau became director of the museum in 1956. The town of Monte Carlo is also perched high on top of the cliffs across the harbor from Monaco-Ville. Monte Carlo is a resort area with a famous gambling casino, many hotels, and lovely flower gardens. It has a reputation as a meeting place for the rich and famous from all over the world.

MONACO

Capital city
Monaco-Ville
(1,800 people)

Area
0.73 square mile
(1.9 sq. km)

Population
29,000 people

Government
Principality

Natural resources
None

Export product
Most income comes from tourism and banking

Unit of money
French franc

Official language
French

N
W ⟶ E
S

Monte-Carlo
CASINO ■

Port of Monaco

La Condamine

MEDITERRANEAN SEA

Monaco-Ville ✪
■ PALACE

Fontvieille

Port of Fontvieille

0	0.5	1	1.5 Mile
0	0.5	1	1.5	2 Kilometers

© 1994 GeoSystems, an R.R. Donnelley & Sons Company

Rainier III became Prince of Monaco in 1949. His full name is Ranier Louis Henri Maxence Bertrand de Grimaldi. His "fairy-tale" marriage to the actress Grace Kelly in 1956 aroused worldwide interest.

With a population of 29,000 in its area of 0.73 square mile (1.9 sq. km), Monaco has a greater population density than any other country in the world (more than 38,000 per square mile or 14,700 per square km).

▲ A portrait in stained glass of St. Benedict, founder of a monastic order in the 500s.

▶ Some early Christians built religious communities called monasteries where they could worship God away from the distractions of daily life. This imaginary model gives an idea of how the early monasteries would have been laid out. It includes an abbey, or church, in which to worship; buildings for living and working; and kitchen gardens for food production.

Monaco's factories produce beer, candy, chemicals, and tobacco. Postage stamps are also an important source of income. But the main industry is tourism. Thousands of visitors arrive every month to enjoy Monaco's beaches and scenery. Since the early 1980s, land has been reclaimed from the sea to extend the seashores.

Many visitors come just for the famous auto races. Drivers from all over the world compete each year in the race known as the Monaco Grand Prix. The race course is only 2 miles (3.2 km) long, but the drivers in the race must circle it 100 times through narrow, winding streets.

More than half of the people of Monaco are French. A small number of people are Monegasque and speak a local dialect—a mixture of French and Italian—also called Monegasque. Many wealthy people from France, Italy, the United States, Britain, and other countries live there, mainly because of Monaco's low taxes.

Monaco has been ruled by the Grimaldi family since the 1200s. Prince Rainier III is the thirty-second Grimaldi to rule.

▶▶▶▶ FIND OUT MORE ◀◀◀◀
Mediterranean Sea

MONASTIC LIFE

A monastery is a building, or a group of buildings, where religious men called *monks* live and work. The word *monastery* comes from a Greek word meaning "living alone." In the early days of the Christian church, Monks lived alone, often spending

time in the desert, thinking about God. Most monks have lived in groups since Saint Benedict's rule in the 500s made monks a kind of family. The chosen leader was given the name of "abbot" from the Hebrew word *abba*, meaning "father," and the monks called each other "brother." Most Christian monks are Roman Catholic. Monasticism also exists in Buddhism and Hinduism. A group of women followed Benedict's rule under the leadership of his twin sister, Saint Scholastica. Such a community came to be called a *convent*, and the women *nuns* or *sisters*. Now there are hundreds of orders of nuns in convents throughout the world.

A Christian monastery sometimes has a *cloister,* or covered walkway, surrounding an open court *(garth)*. There is also a kitchen, a dining hall called a *refectory*, and a *calefactory*, or sitting room. The monks grow their own food in the monastery garden. Often they keep bees for honey and have a well-stocked pond for fresh fish. There may be a guest house and small buildings for crafts.

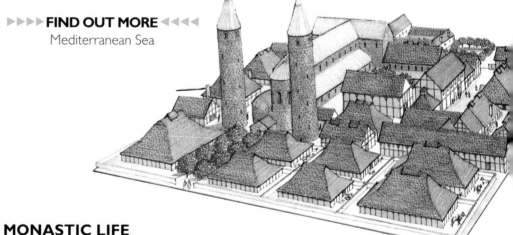

Many monastic orders have schools, colleges, or universities on the grounds. For many centuries, monks have been teachers and scholars.

Monks have always helped their neighbors. They have taught farming, reading, writing, bread making, wine making, and other skills. Monasteries have traditionally taken in the lame and the sick and have given shelter to travelers.

Everyday monastic life is very busy. Much time is spent in prayer, studying, reading the Scriptures, and working at various tasks. Time is set aside for *contemplation*, or silent thought. Some orders of monks observe a vow of silence. In recent years, many communities of monks have relaxed their rules and given up the observance of silence to make their lives more relevant to life today and to be of more service to people. Some monks and nuns no longer live in monasteries or convents and mix more freely with people outside their religious community.

The first monastery was built around A.D. 300 on an island in the Nile River in Egypt by a monk named Pachomius. Saint Augustine, Saint Benedict, and Saint Francis of Assisi founded monastic orders. Today, thousands of men live by the rules laid down by these men, having taken *vows* (holy promises) of poverty, chastity, and obedience.

Some of the earliest monasteries in North America were founded in the 1700s in what is now California by the Spanish Franciscan friar Junípero Serra. Twelve missions were built a day's journey apart. The monks who lived in them helped to spread Christianity among the Native Americans and worked also to educate the people. The first monastery built in the United States was St. Vincent's Arch Abbey, founded by German Benedictine monks at Latrobe, Pennsylvania, in 1846. One of the best known is Gethsemane near Bardstown, Kentucky. Gethsemane is a Trappist monastery where author and poet Thomas Merton (1915–1968) was a monk.

▶ ▶ ▶ ▶ **FIND OUT MORE** ◀ ◀ ◀ ◀
Religion; Roman Catholic Church

MONET, CLAUDE (1840–1926)

The French artist Claude Monet was born in Paris but grew up in Le Havre. He studied with the landscape painter Louis Boudin, who encouraged him to paint outdoor scenes in the open air. Monet went on to the School of Fine Arts in Paris, but he did not like the conventional style of painting taught there. He went back to his old teacher and continued to study. At the time, most painters "jotted down" sketchlike paintings of outdoor scenes and then recreated them in larger, more lifelike finished forms in the studio. Monet broke with tradition by making his sponta-

▲ *The Houses of Parliament, Sunset*, by Claude Monet, **National Gallery of Art, Washington, D.C., Chester Dale collection. It was Monet who accidently gave rise to the name *Impressionists*. He exhibited a painting in 1874 entitled *Impression: Sunrise*. A critical reviewer called the entire show impressionist, which gave the movement its name.**

LEARN BY DOING

Monet felt that shapes were much less important in a painting than color. He enjoyed painting misty scenes in which forms were hard to see. Look at his *The Houses of Parliament*, shown above. The fog rises from the Thames River, and it is hard to make out the exact shapes of the buildings. But the mist creates a mysterious, otherworldly mood. Turn to the article on PARLIAMENT to see another picture of this scene. Do you get different feelings from the painting and the picture? If so, think about why this might be.

▲ **Claude Monet worked outdoors in all kinds of weather. He dismissed the dull tones and somber colors of the orthodox landscapes, seeing his subject in a new light. In 1883, he settled in Giverney, France. His eyesight rapidly failing, it was there that he did the series of *Water lily* paintings.**

Claude Monet liked painting the same subject again and again. He painted Rouen Cathedral 20 times, in different kinds of weather and at different times of day.

neous impressions the finished work.

Painting landscapes outdoors in natural, changing light became the most important subject for Monet. It remained so for the rest of his long life as a painter. He became the leader of a group of painters in Paris who became known as *Impressionists.*

In 1876, he did a series of paintings of scenes in a Paris railway station. The crowds, the steaming engines, the glass roof, and the brilliant sky provided Monet with dramatic color contrasts. He was always most interested in the effects of outdoor light and atmosphere. Sometimes he would paint several pictures showing the same subject in different kinds of light. Once he created 15 paintings of the same haystack.

Monet had a hard time making his living as an artist. He was more than 40 years old before he was able to buy a house and some land in Giverny, near Vernon. There he built a Japanese garden and a lily pond. Water lilies became one of his favorite subjects.

▶▶▶▶ **FIND OUT MORE** ◀◀◀◀
Impressionism

MONEY

Suppose you bought some candy for 20¢ and gave the shopkeeper a dollar. Think how surprised you would be if, instead of 80 cents in change, he or she gave you 10 shells, 15 beads, 2 small animal skins, and a shark's tooth! All of these things have at some time been used as money. Money is based on the idea of *value*. People place a value on things that they want and on things that are rare or hard to get. Diamonds, for example, are scarce and have a high value because many people want them. If no one wanted diamonds, they would be worth very little. On the other hand, people do not place a high value on sand. It is easy to get, and a ton of it can be bought for only a few dollars.

Barter
Before money was developed, people used to trade by *bartering*. In bartering, people exchanged goods. A pottery maker who wanted 1 yard (1 m) of woolen cloth might pay for it by giving the weaver two storage jars. The weaver might pay his or her assistant one jar for two days' work.

Mediums of Exchange
In some places, certain goods—furs, shells, metals, oxen, and others—became the *medium of exchange*. All goods were given a value that was related to the medium of exchange. A plow might be worth 20 beaver furs, a horse might be worth 50 furs, and a piece of land might be worth 300 furs. Mediums of exchange were the earliest kind of money, and they all had three characteristics in common: For one reason or another, people wanted them. They could be used over and over again for a fairly long period of time, and they were easy to identify. Grain does not make good money because it gets eaten or spoils.

Metals, such as gold, silver, copper, bronze, nickel, and iron, were also used as mediums of exchange, but not in the form of coins. The metals were in powder form or made up into *ingots*, or bars, that had to be weighed each time something was bought or sold. Eventually, metals became the main medium of exchange.

Coin Money

The earliest known coins were made in Lydia, a little country in what is now Turkey. King Croesus, the ruler, had the coins made of *electrum* (a mixture of gold and silver). Coins were easier to use than ingots because they could be counted instead of weighed. Each coin had a certain size and was given a certain value depending on the amount of the metal it contained. When money is given a value that is equal to the value of the material it is made of, it is called *commodity money*. Commodity money is no longer used in the United States.

Because coins were not weighed, people sometimes cheated by cutting some of the metal off the edges. This lowered the coin's value. To prevent this, little grooves were placed

▲ The Sumerians from Mesopotamia used clay tokens for trading. It is thought there were different tokens for each commodity being traded.

▲ Chinese money was knife-shaped to begin with, but gradually became more round.

Paper money is not commodity money, because the paper itself is not worth the amount printed on it. Paper money began as *credit money*. Credit money represents a certain amount of gold or other medium of exchange. If U.S. dollars were credit money, you could exchange a $5 bill at a bank and get $5 worth of gold.

U.S. currency used to be credit money, but nowadays it cannot be exchanged for gold. U.S. currency, like that of many other countries, is *fiat money*. Fiat money cannot be exchanged for gold. Its value is determined by the government. The government simply states that this money is the only type that can be used as *legal tender*. Legal tender is the official money of a country and must be used for making payments and settling debts. It must be accepted by those to whom it is offered.

▲ Old Spanish dollars were known as "pieces of eight." They were often cut into eight bits. Two bits, or a quarter, were commonly used.

► An ancient coin minted in Greece in 412 B.C. to commemorate a victory.

on the edges of high-value coins. A trimmed coin could then be identified by its lack of grooves. You can see these grooves on U. S. dimes, quarters, and half-dollars.

Paper Money

Most of the money used today is paper money. Paper money is even handier than coins. A $20 bill is easier to carry around and keep track of than 80 quarters would be. Also, people do not try to trim paper money, because the paper trimmings are not worth anything.

Checks and Credit Cards

Today, many people use checks and credit cards in place of cash. When someone writes a check payable to you, he or she is giving you a certain amount of money deposited in a bank. You can take the check to a bank and receive cash. When you

▲ The use of paper money began in China in the 700s. Marco Polo wrote about it in the 1200s. This note from the 1300s is made of bark paper.

WHERE TO DISCOVER MORE

Cribb, Joe. *Money*. New York: Alfred A. Knopf, Inc., 1990.

Kyte, Kathleen Sharar. *The Kids' Complete Guide to Money*. New York: Alfred A. Knopf, Inc., 1984.

QUIZ

1. What is *electrum*?

2. Is U.S. money *credit money*, *fiat money*, or *legal tender*?

3. Whose picture is on a five-dollar bill?

4. Who are the only Presidents to appear on both a coin and a bill?

(Answers on page 1792)

▼ **Notes carry a lot of information. The two signatures are from the Treasurer and Secretary of the Treasury; the two seals represent the Treasury and the Federal Reserve district.**

buy something with a credit card, you are making a promise to pay later when the bill is sent to you.

United States Money

When settlers came to America from Europe, they brought copper, silver, and gold coins from their home countries. Coins of many countries were used in the colonies. Some of these were "pieces of eight"—the name for Spanish dollars of that time. One piece of eight was worth eight smaller coins, called *reals* or *bits*. Some people still say "two bits" to mean a quarter.

The first coins actually made in America were threepence (three penny), sixpence, and twelvepence pieces, issued in 1652 in the Massachusetts Bay colony. During the American Revolution, the Continental Congress issued paper money. Because this currency could not be exchanged for gold or silver, people stopped using it, and it soon became worthless.

The Constitution of the United States gave Congress the right to *coin* (produce and distribute) money and control its value. On April 2, 1792, Congress established the United States Mint. The mint began to make copper, silver, and gold coins in Philadelphia, Pennsylvania. These coins included copper cents and half-cents, silver dimes, half-dimes, quarters, half-dollars, dollars, two-

and-one-half dollar gold quarter-eagles, five-dollar gold half-eagles, and ten-dollar gold eagles. Later, the mint made two-cent, three-cent, and twenty-cent coins. Nickels were made in 1866 to replace the half-dime. Today's U. S. coins, like the paper money, are fiat money. The metal in a coin is not worth the amount on the coin. In the late 1960s, the federal government stopped making silver quarters and dimes to save silver. The metal was changed to a layer of copper sandwiched between two layers of nickel.

The first denominations of paper money printed by the United States Government were $5, $10, and $20 bills, which were made in 1861. The backs of the bills were printed in green and people called them "greenbacks," a term still used today to denote money. Paper money in a greater variety of values was issued by Congress in 1862. The values ranged from $1 to $10,000. However, since 1969, bills for $500, $1,000, $5,000, and $10,000 are no longer issued.

Private banks in the United States and elsewhere used to issue their own notes, which could be *redeemed* (cashed in) for gold or silver, but they have given up doing this.

▶▶▶▶ **FIND OUT MORE** ◀◀◀◀
Banks and Banking; Coins; Economics; International Trade

MONGOLIA

The "Land of the Blue Skies" is one of the least-known countries in the world. Mongolia lies between Russia and China in east central Asia. It is officially called the State of Mongolia and unofficially Outer Mongolia. A region to the south, called Inner Mongolia, is part of China. More than 700 years ago, Mongolia was the center of the great empire of the Mongol leader Ghengis Khan.

Printing plate No.   Seal   Hero's portrait   Bank   Seal   Bill No.

Value   Signature   Value   Year of design   Signature

Mongolia is a vast country, more than twice the size of Texas. But much of the land is barren and desolate. The flat, rocky wastes of the Gobi Desert cover a large area of south-eastern Mongolia. A few of the rare Prze-walski's horses, the oldest living type of wild horse, are found in the desert. Farther north is a region of grassy plains, or *steppes*. The land rises in the west to forested hills and the rugged Altai Mountains. This area is rich in wildlife, with animals such as ermine, sable, otters, moose, and musk deer. Mongolia has many extremes in climate. In the north, the temperature in winter can fall to 50°F below zero (-45°C). In the south, it can rise to 107°F (42°C) in the summer. Rainfall is very light.

Some Mongols still follow a *nomadic*, or wandering, life, herding animals. The herders and their families live in round felt tents on wooden frames, known as *yurts*. These are folded and packed on the backs of camels as the herders move from place to place in search of grass and water.

Many Mongols now live on state farms, controlled by the government. They herd livestock or grow grain. Fur trapping is an important industry in the mountains, and coal is mined. Textiles, leather, meat, and grain are processed in factories. The religion of most Mongols is Lamaism, or

MONGOLIA

Capital city
Ulaanbaatar
(500,000 people)

Area
604,250 square miles
(1,565,000 sq. km)

Population
2,150,000 people

Government
Multiparty republic

Natural resources
Coal, copper, phosphates, zinc, molybdenum, tin, tungsten, nickel, fluorspar, gold

Export products
Livestock, animal products, wool, hides, fluorspar, minerals

Unit of money
Tugrik

Official language
Mongolian

◀ Mongolian nomads herd sheep, camels, horses, and yaks. The animals in the herd provide milk and meat for food, hair for tent covering, and hides for leather articles. Children learn at an early age to ride the tough, fast Mongol ponies. Mongols meet annually for horse races in the capital of Ulaanbaatar.

▲ Mongolian herdsmen lay the foundations for a circular tent, or *yurt*. These suit their wandering lifestyle, as they can be put up and taken down quite quickly.

MONITOR AND MERRIMACK

The famous battle between the *Monitor* and the *Merrimack* in 1862 was the first encounter in history between ironclad warships. This battle was the beginning of the end of wooden warships. It was also one of the first sea battles between ships powered by steam.

During the Civil War, the Confederates wanted to break the Union naval blockade along their seacoast. In the spring of 1862, they raised the frigate *Merrimack*, which had been sunk. They rebuilt it into an ironclad vessel. They covered the ship's sides with sloping 4-inch (10-cm) iron plates and placed a strong iron ram on its bow. The ship's name was officially changed to *Virginia*, but people still called it the *Merrimack*.

The strange looking warship sailed into Hampton Roads, Virginia, on March 8, 1862, to shell the wooden ships of the Union fleet anchored there. These ships could not damage the ironclad sides of the *Merrimack*. Their shots bounced off like harmless pebbles. Before leaving because of low tide, the *Merrimack* destroyed two Union ships. The captain planned to return the next day. His idea was to bombard the rest of the Northern fleet and sail up the Potomac River to shell the capital city, Washington. However, when the captain sailed into Hampton Roads the next day, he was faced with a

Tibetan Buddhism. In Ulaanbaatar, the capital, is an ancient monastery where ten thousand Buddhist monks once lived.

In the 1300s, Mongolia began to lose the great power it had enjoyed during the time of Genghis Khan and his descendants. Kublai Khan, a grandson of Genghis, had conquered China and ruled lands stretching from the Pacific Ocean to the Black Sea in Europe. The Manchus, an east Asian people who later conquered China in the 1600s, extended their rule over Outer Mongolia. In 1921, with the help of the former Soviet Union, Outer Mongolia established itself as an independent state—the State of Mongolia. It was ruled by a Communist government. In 1992, democracy was introduced with a market economy.

▶▶▶▶ **FIND OUT MORE** ◀◀◀◀
Beijing; China; Genghis Khan; Polo, Marco

▶ The historic battle between the *Monitor* (left) and the *Merrimack* (right). When the *Monitor* was built, its curious appearance prompted one observer to describe it as "a cheese box on a raft." But it was a lot easier to maneuver than the *Merrimack*. However, neither ship was able to sink the other in this battle.

warship even stranger looking than the *Merrimack*. It was the *Monitor*, another ironclad ship.

The *Monitor* was designed for the Union navy by a Swedish engineer John Ericsson. It was constructed partly of iron and partly of wood. Its sides were covered with iron 5 inches (13 cm) thick. A gun turret rose from its deck, which was flat and raftlike, almost level with the water. The turret could turn completely around in a circle and was armed with 11-inch (28-cm) guns.

The two ships faced each other in combat for almost four hours. They shelled each other time after time, but neither could do much damage to the other. The battle was inconclusive, though both sides claimed victory when it finally ended.

Neither ship lasted long after the historic battle. In May 1862, the Confederates blew up the *Merrimack* when they abandoned Norfolk. In December 1862, the *Monitor* sank in rough seas during a violent storm off Cape Hatteras, North Carolina.

But the battle between the *Monitor* and the *Merrimack* was an encounter that changed naval warfare.

▶▶▶▶ **FIND OUT MORE** ◀◀◀◀
Civil War; Navy

MONKEY

Monkeys, apes, and human beings are all primates. They may all be descended from the same ancestor— a tiny, furry animal that lived millions of years ago.

Today, monkeys are classified into two main groups. *New World* monkeys live in the jungles of South America, Mexico, and Central America. *Old World* monkeys live in the jungles of Africa, India, and Southeast Asia. Nearly all monkeys eat insects, leaves, and fruit, although some

▲ Some monkeys from the Old and New Worlds. Monkeys are among the noisiest and liveliest of the jungle creatures. They usually live up in the *canopy* (top of the trees) and swing from branch to branch with ease.

species eat only leaves and some species eat meat. Most monkeys live in trees, but a few species live on the ground. Monkeys usually live in pairs (male and female) or in groups. Some species are only a few inches in height; others are several feet tall. All monkeys are very good parents.

Some New World monkeys have *prehensile* (grasping) tails. That is, they can use their tails as extra hands—to hang onto branches or to hold things with. Old World monkeys cannot use their tails in this way. In fact, some Old World monkeys do not even have tails. A New World monkey's face looks flat. Its cheeks and nose look as if they have been pushed in. The noses of Old World monkeys stick out more. Old World monkeys can also stretch their cheeks, as you do when you fill your mouth with food or air. They often use those stretchable cheeks for storing food. Old World monkeys have 32 teeth, the same number that human beings have. Most New World monkeys have 36 teeth. Old World monkeys also have thick pads, or

▲ The squirrel monkey of South American rain forests feeds on insects as well as flowers, nuts, and fruit.

▲ The noisiest of all monkeys is the howling monkey of South America. In the males, a bone at the top of the windpipe has developed to form a resonant sound box. The howls, which keep other monkeys away, can be heard great distances.

The Barbary apes on Gibraltar are not really apes but monkeys of the macaque family. They were once supposed to have warned the British by barking when the Spanish made a surprise attack. It is believed that Britain will never lose Gibraltar as long as the apes remain there.

calluses, growing on their buttocks to sit on. The calluses are often brightly colored. New World monkeys do not have these calluses.

Some New World Monkeys

Howling monkeys can scream very loudly. They can be heard for miles. Sometimes these monkeys will howl together at sunrise or sunset. Howlers, which are some of the largest monkeys, are several feet long. But their brains are small and poorly developed.

Capuchin monkeys are the cleverest of the New World monkeys. They are also called "organ grinder" monkeys because street musicians with hand organs once trained them to collect money. Capuchin monkeys live in the jungle and travel in large groups, chattering and talking among themselves. People in the jungle do not like them. The capuchins are always stealing chickens from the people and eating fruit and vegetables from their gardens.

Spider monkeys have long, thin bodies and very long, strong tails. They use their tails to hold onto things more than any other kind of monkey does. The spider monkey received its name because it can hang from a branch by its tail, like a spider at the end of its thread. Spider monkeys can also grab food with their tails when the food is too far away to get with their hands. They are the best climbers in the jungle, although they do not have thumbs.

Marmosets are a family of small monkeys with fine, soft fur covering their bodies. An adult marmoset is about the size of a squirrel. But the pygmy marmoset grows to only 6 inches (15 cm). Most of them live along the Amazon River in South America. Unlike other New World monkeys, marmosets have only 32 teeth, and they cannot use their tails as extra hands. They have claws on the ends of their fingers and toes instead of fingernails and toenails.

▲ Forest monkeys like the bearded sakis from South America are in danger of extinction, as more and more forests are being cut down for lumber or are undergoing cultivation.

Some Old World Monkeys

Macaques are found everywhere in Africa, India, and Southeast Asia and also in some areas of the New World. One kind of macaque, called the Barbary ape, lives on the Rock of Gibraltar in southern Europe. The kind of macaque found in India is called the rhesus monkey. This monkey is sacred in the Hindu religion. Scientists often use the rhesus monkey in medical experiments.

Macaques, like other Old World monkeys, live in large groups called *troops.* Each troop has an old male macaque as a leader. The leader always goes ahead of the troop. He looks out for danger and searches for things to eat. If the leader finds an orchard, a cornfield, or a vegetable garden, all the macaques eat as much as they can. If the leader sees anyone coming, he gives a warning cry. The members of the troop then fill their cheeks with extra food and run for the nearest group of trees. The macaques do a great deal of damage to crops and are not very popular with the farmers.

Baboons and *mandrills* are the largest and fiercest of all monkeys. They are about the size of a large dog. Some male baboons can weigh up to 100 pounds (45 kg). Like dogs, they have long snouts with very strong jaws and big teeth. Mandrills have bright blue cheeks and a long, flat red nose. These colored stripes on their faces become brighter when the mandrills are excited. Baboons and mandrills live on the ground in large troops. There might be as many as 100 members in one troop. A troop of baboons is led by the old males. The males stand guard at night and watch out for danger. They also lead the troop on expeditions for food. If a leopard, a lion, or a tiger tries to attack a member of the troop, all the males will attack the animal together. The males may even kill the animal. Baboons and mandrills are not afraid of animals, including human beings.

▶ ▶ ▶ ▶ **FIND OUT MORE** ◀ ◀ ◀ ◀
Ape; Claws and Nails;
Hands and Feet; Lemur; Mammal

▲ **The West African mandrill is the largest of the monkeys, with a head and body length of more than 3 feet (1 m). Its nimble fingers can gather food easily.**

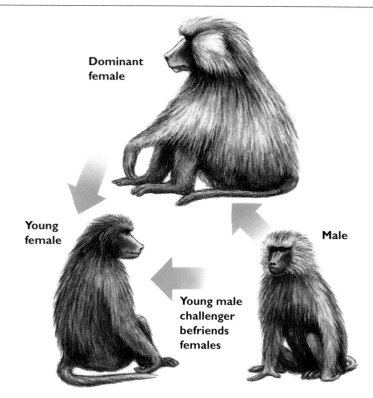

Dominant female

Young female

Male

Young male challenger befriends females

MONORAIL

SEE RAILROAD;
TRANSPORTATION

MONROE, JAMES (1758–1831)

The fifth President of the United States is best remembered for a statement he made in his annual message to Congress in December 1823. Several Spanish colonies in South America had recently declared their independence. President Monroe announced that any attempt by European powers to set up new colonies in any part of the Americas would be considered an unfriendly act by the United States. This warning, part of the statement known as the *Monroe Doctrine*, became an important part of American foreign policy.

Monroe was born on a small plantation in eastern Virginia. He became a student at the College of William and Mary but left at the age of 17 to fight in the American Revolution. The following year, he was commissioned a lieutenant by General

▲ **Baboons live in troops with a complicated social system. At the top is a senior female and her young, followed by her grown-up daughters and their young. A male newcomer befriends females and challenges other males within the troop.**

When James Monroe was President, the population of the United States was just over 11 million people.

JAMES MONROE, FIFTH PRESIDENT

MARCH 4, 1817– MARCH 4, 1825

Born: April 18, 1758, Westmoreland County, Virginia

Parents: Spence and Elizabeth Jones Monroe

Education: College of William and Mary, Williamsburg, Virginia

Religion: Episcopalian

Occupation: Lawyer

Political party: Democratic-Republican

State represented: Virginia

Married: 1786 to Elizabeth Kortright (1768–1830)

Children: Two daughters

Died: July 4, 1831, New York City

Buried: Hollywood Cemetery, Richmond, Virginia

George Washington. Monroe was wounded at the Battle of Trenton, but he recovered and rose to the rank of lieutenant colonel. He served in both the Continental Army and the Virginia militia. During the war, he met Thomas Jefferson, under whom he later studied law. Although not a brilliant student, young Monroe was hardworking and sincere. "He is a man whose soul might be turned wrong side outwards," said Jefferson, "without discovering a blemish to the world."

The qualities of honesty and courage that had won Thomas Jefferson's admiration made James Monroe popular with the voters of Virginia, and they elected him to several important public offices. He served as a United States senator and twice as governor of Virginia. In 1786, he married Elizabeth Kortright, a beautiful young lady from New York.

President George Washington appointed Monroe United States minister to France in 1794. Nine years later, after Jefferson became President, Monroe was again sent to France. He helped another United States minister, Robert R. Livingston, to arrange for the purchase of the vast American territory known as Louisiana from France. The success of this mission showed Monroe to be a skillful diplomat. After that, he served as minister to Great Britain, as governor of Virginia for a second time, and as secretary of state. At that time, he tried to reach agreement with Britain over the impressment of American seamen. However, he soon saw that war was inevitable. During the War of 1812, he held the office of Secretary of State and Secretary of War simultaneously. In 1816, Monroe was elected President of the United States.

Monroe became President at a time when industry was beginning to flourish in the Northern states, and new frontiers were being carved out in the West. It was a peaceful and prosperous time for the country. No bitter political fights were taking place, and the country was expanding to the West.

James Monroe was a likable gentleman, whose years in the Presidency were called the "Era of Good Feelings." But an important issue arose near the end of his first administration—the question of slavery. The country was becoming divided over this question. Monroe privately agreed with the slaveowners, but his chief aim was to keep the country united. In 1820, he agreed to the so-called Missouri Compromise. This agreement, made in Congress, allowed slavery in the new state of Missouri, but forbade it in any other part of the Louisiana Territory. During this time, the United States' borders were extended to the south, after the purchase of Florida from Spain in 1819.

In 1820, Monroe ran for reelection with no opponents. During his second term, the attention of most Americans was turned to the revolutionary wars in South America. It was then that Monroe issued his famous warning to European nations, which came to be known as the Monroe Doctrine.

Monroe's presidency ended in 1825, and he retired to his Oak Hill estate in Virginia. After his wife died, he spent his last year with one of his daughters in New York City.

▶▶▶▶ **FIND OUT MORE** ◀◀◀◀
Louisiana Purchase; Missouri; Monroe Doctrine; Slavery; War of 1812

MONROE DOCTRINE

On December 2, 1823, President James Monroe sent a message to Congress stating that the continents of North and South America shall never again "be considered as sub-

jects for future colonization by any European powers." He also made it clear that the United States would consider any attempt by European nations to interfere in the affairs of any country of the Western Hemisphere as a direct threat to the peace and safety of the United States.

In 1815, the leaders of Russia, Austria, and Prussia had joined in what was called a "Holy Alliance." President Monroe believed that the Holy Alliance would support Spain's efforts to regain control of its former South American colonies. His message to Congress was a warning to the European nations that the United States would come to the aid of any other country in the Western Hemisphere.

The Monroe Doctrine, worked out by Secretary of State John Quincy Adams, was later regarded unfavorably by Latin American countries. They felt that it meant the United States could interfere in their affairs. In the 1920s and 1930s, Presidents Hoover and Roosevelt added the idea of the "Good Neighbor Policy" to the Monroe Doctrine. This meant that the United States would not interfere in Latin American politics—just as Europe had been told not to interfere before.

▶▶▶▶ **FIND OUT MORE** ◀◀◀◀
Colony; International Relations; Monroe, James

▲ **James Monroe explains the details of the Monroe Doctrine to his colleagues. The doctrine became an important part of foreign policy.**

 ## MONSOON

The word *monsoon* comes from the Arabic word for "season." A monsoon is a wind that blows from land to sea during one season (winter), and from sea to land during another season (summer). It occurs mainly in southern Asia.

Monsoons are caused by differences in temperature between the land and sea. During the summer, the earth takes in a lot of heat from the summer sun, warming the air above the land. When the summer monsoons blow, cool air from over the sea blows toward the land. This cool air also carries moisture from the sea, and rain falls over the land. Summer monsoons are called "wet monsoons." Summer monsoons bring the "rainy season." For example, Allahabad, India, and Washington, D.C., get the same amount of rainfall over a full year. In Washington, rain falls equally throughout the year. But in Allahabad, most of the rain falls during the summer monsoons—in June, July, August, and September.

During the winter, the land grows cooler than the sea. The cool air then blows from the land toward the sea. Winter monsoons are called "dry

▼ **The monsoon winds bring very heavy seasonal rainfall to India. Cherrapunji holds the record for the most rain in one month—354 inches (9,000 mm). In winter, the winds reverse, blowing from the land to the sea, and rainfall becomes scarce over much of the subcontinent.**

Inches of rain

	More than 175
	100–175
	50–100
	25–50
	12.5–25
	2.5–12.5
	Below 2.5

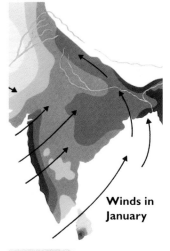

Winds in January

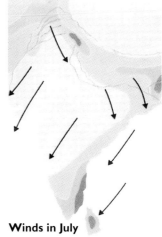

Winds in July

▲ Tutunendo in South America has the highest average yearly rainfall, 463½ inches (11,770 mm).

Since ancient times, sailors have used the seasonal changes of the monsoon winds on their voyages. Ships in the Arabian Sea sail westward from India to Africa when the monsoon blows toward the southwest. In summer, the monsoon blows from the southwest, and the trading vessels return to India.

▼ Montana's grasslands are good for grazing cattle. Clear streams, such as this one near Ronan, attract many trout fishermen. In the background is the spectacular Mission Range.

monsoons." In China, the winter monsoon brings dust storms. The air blowing to the sea carries yellowish dust from the dry land. The dust fills the air for weeks at a time, sifting through windows and covering everything. Chinese farmers have been known to attach sails to wheelbarrows for the monsoon to push.

▶ ▶ ▶ ▶ FIND OUT MORE ◀ ◀ ◀ ◀
Weather; Wind

MONTANA

The name *Montana* comes from a Spanish word meaning "mountainous." Western Montana is a very mountainous region that contains Glacier National Park. The park is one of the places where you can see the Rocky Mountains at their best. It is a wilderness of steep, wooded slopes and flowery mountain meadows. Streams tumble over waterfalls. Blue lakes lie in peaceful valleys. High in the mountains are *glaciers*. A glacier is a great sheet of ice that moves slowly down a slope or valley.

Glacier National Park has more than 60 glaciers. This park was established in 1910 and contains 1,031,129 acres (417,298 ha).

The park has other wonders, too. One of them is Triple Divide Peak. This mountain rises about 1½ miles (2.4 km) above sea level. Its name gives you a hint as to what makes it unusual. The streams that run down its slopes flow in three directions. On the western side, the water drains into rivers bound for the Pacific Ocean. On the eastern side, some water flows north, finally reaching the cold Hudson Bay in Canada. The water that flows south ends up in the warm Gulf of Mexico.

The Land and Climate
Triple Divide Park stands on the Continental Divide, the high ridges of the Rocky Mountains. The Rockies cover the western two-fifths of Montana. They spread into Idaho on the west and southwest and into Wyoming in the south. Montana's northern Rockies extend into Canada. Across the border from Glacier National Park is Canada's Waterton Lakes National Park. Together, the two form the International Peace Park.

East of the Rockies in Montana lie the Great Plains. These rolling plains span the Canadian border in the north and the Wyoming border in the south. They are highest at the foot of the Rockies. They slope downward into North Dakota in the east. The broad horizons of the Great Plains give Montana the nickname "Big Sky Country." The plains are dotted with hills and crossed by rivers. Most of these flow into the Missouri River.

Winters can be very cold in Montana. Not just in the high mountains but on the plains also. Icy winds from Canada sweep across them. These winds often bring blizzards. A warm, dry wind called a *chinook* sometimes blows down the eastern

MONTANA

Capital
Helena
(24,569 people)

Area
147,138 square miles
(381,058 sq. km)
Rank 4th

Population
799,065 people
Rank 44th

Statehood
November 8, 1889
(41st state admitted)

Principal rivers
Missouri River
Yellowstone River

Highest point
Granite Peak;
12,799 feet (3,901 m)

Largest city
Billings (81,151 people)

Motto
Oro y Plata
(Gold and Silver)

Song
"Montana"

Famous people
Gary Cooper, Will James,
Myrna Loy, Mike Mansfield,
Jeannette Rankin

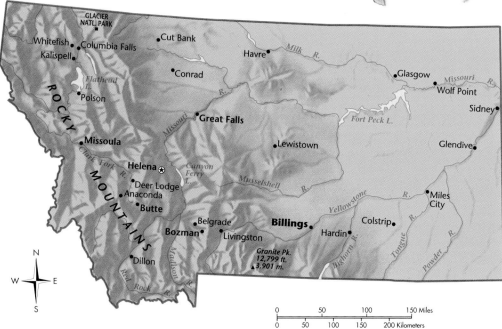

GLACIER NATL. PARK
Whitefish
Columbia Falls
Kalispell
Cut Bank
Havre
Milk R.
Conrad
Glasgow
Missouri R.
Wolf Point
Flathead L.
Polson
Sidney
ROCKY
Missouri
Great Falls
Fort Peck L.
Missoula
Lewistown
Glendive
Clark Fork R.
Helena ☆
Canyon Ferry L.
Deer Lodge
Musselshell R.
Anaconda
Butte
MOUNTAINS
Belgrade
Billings
Colstrip
Yellowstone R.
Miles City
Bozman
Livingston
Hardin
Dillon
Madison R.
Granite Pk.
12,799 ft.
▲ 3,901 m.
Bighorn R.
Tongue R.
Powder R.
Red Rock R.

N
W E
S

0   50   100   150 Miles
0   50   100   150   200 Kilometers
© 1994 GeoSystems, an R.R. Donnelley & Sons Company

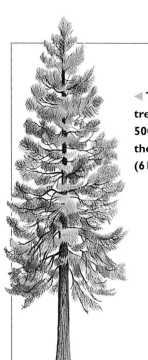

STATE SYMBOLS

◀ The ponderosa pine tree can live up to 500 years. It grows to the height of 200 feet (61 m).

▲ The western meadowlark became the state bird on January 4, 1931.

▲ The pick, shovel, and plow represent the mining and farming of the pioneer times.

▶ The root of the bitterroot was once a valuable part of the Native American diet.

Except for Alaska and Wyoming, Montana has fewer people per square mile than any other state: 5.7 (2.2 per sq. km).

slopes of the Rockies. The temperatures can suddenly rise more than 50°F (30°C)! Chinooks make the winter weather milder and often melt away snow. Summers are cool in the mountains, but hot in the plains.

Precipitation is generally light throughout the state. The mountains have enough moisture for trees to grow. But the plains are much drier. The chief vegetation on the plains is grass. It grows in bunches on the bare earth. Except in late spring, the grass is more yellow than green.

History

The Native Americans had Montana completely to themselves before 1700. The Flathead tribes lived in the western mountain valleys. The Blackfoot and Crow tribes held most of the plains area. The Flatheads hunted deer and elk in the mountains. They trapped otters and other fur-bearing animals and fished for trout in the rivers and lakes. The plains tribes hunted buffalo (bison). They hunted on foot before white men brought horses to North America. Buffalo meat was the main food of these Native Americans. They made clothing and *tepees* from buffalo hides.

The first white people in Montana

▲ The spectacular scenery of the sheer cliffs at Devil Canyon, seen from the overlook at Bighorn Canyon.

were French. They came from New France (French Canada) about 1740. Most of Montana was sold to the United States by France as part of the Louisiana Purchase in 1803. An American party led by Meriwether Lewis and William Clark was then sent to explore the area. These men traveled up the Missouri River to Montana in 1804. They were on their way to the Pacific. Clark explored the Yellowstone River on the return trip. Lewis and Clark returned to St. Louis, Missouri, in 1806. People there were greatly interested in what the explorers said about the unknown West. A Missouri fur trader named Manuel Lisa was especially interested. He took some men up the Yellowstone River in 1807 and built Montana's first trading post at the point where the Bighorn River meets the Yellowstone. The fur trade was Montana's earliest industry.

A priest-pioneer arrived in the region in 1840. He was Father Pierre Jean de Smet from Belgium. He and

▼ An almost deserted street in the heat of a summer's afternoon in Livingstone, a town in southern Montana.

several other priests founded a mission in the valley of the Bitterroot River. The priests taught the Flathead tribes about Christianity and also taught them European farming methods. The first crops grown in Montana in the white people's way were the potatoes, wheat, and oats planted at the mission.

Gold was discovered at Grasshopper Creek in southwestern Montana during the Civil War. Miners rushed there and took out $10 million worth of gold in a single year. This was the beginning of Montana's mining industry. Silver was found north of the gold region in 1875. The city of Butte sprang up near the gold mines. Later, silver and copper were discovered there.

The Wild West was truly wild in those days. Robbings and killings were common in Montana. Native Americans became alarmed as more and more white people arrived. They feared the loss of their hunting grounds. Some tribes fought the settlers and the United States Army in the 1870s. General George Custer and his entire command of 265 soldiers were killed at the Little Big Horn River on June 25, 1876. The Native Americans won many battles, but they lost the war to the whites. They were forced to live on reservations. There are now Blackfoot, Crow, Sioux, and Cheyenne settled on seven reservations.

As more people came to Montana, the need for food increased. Soon the grass that had fed the buffalo was feeding cattle and sheep. Crops were planted in mountain valleys and on the plains.

Working in Montana
Today, agriculture is Montana's most important business. Cattle raising is still widespread. Much of Montana's farming is carried out by irrigation in river valleys. But the leading crop, wheat, is raised by a method called *dry farming*. Wheat farmers raise a crop only every second year. Moisture builds up in the soil, and the farmers can use two years' rain to grow one year's crop.

Manufacturing is the state's second largest business. Timber from mountain forests provides raw material for the state's chief product—lumber. Farm products are processed into sugar, flour, and meal. The third biggest business is mining. Oil, copper, and coal now earn the most money in this industry. Tourism is also an important source of income. Camping, fishing, hunting, horseback riding, mountain climbing, and skiing are available. People can tour mines near Butte and visit Native American reservations.

▶▶▶▶ **FIND OUT MORE** ◀◀◀◀
Bison; Blackfoot; Custer, George Armstrong; Fur; Glacier; Lewis and Clark Expedition

MONTENEGRO

SEE YUGOSLAVIA

MONTH

Our calendar, the system we use to tell the time of year, is made up of days, weeks, months, and years. Originally, a month was the period between one new moon and another, about 29½ days. This is a *lunar month*. The word *month* comes from moon. Most people in the Western world today use the *Gregorian* calendar, invented by Pope Gregory XIII in the 1580s. Our months vary from 28 to 31 days each. Every four years an extra day is added to February to make our calendar fit the solar calendar. (The amount of time it takes the Earth to go all the way around the sun is 365¼ days.) The calendar

Grasshopper glacier, near Cooke City, Montana, was named for the great numbers of grasshoppers trapped in the ice a long time ago. The grasshoppers can still be seen today.

▼ The emperor Julius Caesar was a great military leader, statesman, and writer. He reformed the calendar and gave his name to our seventh month, July.

▲ In France, in 1793, the months were given new names. February (top) became Ventose; November (below) became Frimaire.

▼ Modern skyscrapers dominate the Montreal skyline. When lit up they present a spectacular sight.

of the ancient Egyptians had 12 months of 30 days each. The first Roman calendar had only ten months and began with *Martius* (March), named for Mars, god of war. Then came *Aprilis* (April), from the Latin *aperire*, "to open"; *Maius* (May), probably from Mala, goddess of spring; and *Iunius* (June), maybe from Juno, goddess of marriage. The other Roman months received their names from the Latin numbers five through ten. *Quintilis*, the fifth month, was changed to *Julius* (July), in honor of Julius Caesar; and *Sextilis*, to *Augustus* (August), in honor of Augustus Caesar. The Romans later added *Ianuarius* (January), named for Janus, a god whose two faces looked backward and forward; and *Februarius* (February), from the Latin *februare*, meaning "to purify."

The French Revolutionary Calendar, used in France from 1793 to 1805, had seasonal names for the 12 months. These names were vintage, fog, sleet, snow, rain, wind, seed, blossom, pasture, harvest, heat, and fruit.

▶ ▶ ▶ ▶ **FIND OUT MORE** ◀ ◀ ◀ ◀
Calendar; Moon
See articles on each month

MONTICELLO

SEE JEFFERSON, THOMAS

MONTREAL

The first European to visit the site of present-day Montreal, Canada, was a Frenchman, Jacques Cartier. In 1535, Cartier explored an island inhabited by more than a thousand Native North Americans who welcomed him warmly. He named a mountain on the island "Mont Real" (Mount Royal). The modern city of Montreal, located on the St. Lawrence River in southern Quebec, is built around Mount Royal. Twelve bridges span the river to connect Montreal with the mainland.

A hundred years passed after Cartier's visit before Montreal was permanently settled by the French. Development of the settlement was greatly hindered by frequent tribal attacks. During the 1700s, the town became a center of the fur trade.

Today, Montreal is the largest city (in population) in Canada and the second largest French-speaking city in the world. (Paris is first.) More than 3 million people live in and around Montreal. About two-thirds of the city's people are of French descent. Both French and English are spoken.

Oil refining and food processing (canned goods, sugar, and beer) are the leading industries. Much clothing, transportation equipment, electrical machinery, steel, and plastics are also manufactured in Montreal. The city has a fine subway (the Metro); a large international airport; a renowned symphony orchestra; outstanding museums and universities; and professional hockey, football, and baseball teams.

▶ ▶ ▶ ▶ **FIND OUT MORE** ◀ ◀ ◀ ◀
Canada; Quebec

MOON

When Neil Armstrong and Edwin Aldrin stepped onto the surface of the moon on July 20, 1969, they were fulfilling an ancient dream of a voyage to the moon. The moon has been a source of wonder and fear for thousands of years. A *lunar eclipse* (when the Earth is directly between the moon and the sun) and a *solar eclipse* (when the moon is directly between the Earth and the sun) often frightened people who did not understand what was happening. But people have learned a great deal about the moon, both from what they have seen through giant telescopes and from information brought back by spacecraft and samples collected by the Apollo 11 astronauts.

Origin of the Moon

Most of the planets in our solar system have satellites—smaller bodies that travel in a constant orbit around them. Some planets have several satellites. Mercury and Venus have none. The Earth has only one natural satellite—the moon. There are several *theories* (ideas) about the origin of the moon. The most widely held theory is that the moon was formed from the same *nebula* (gas cloud) that formed the sun, the Earth, and the other planets and their moons. As the gas cloud grew smaller, particles constantly collided and clung together to form the planets and their satellites. Other scientists believe that the moon once had its own orbit around the sun. It came within the Earth's gravitational range and was pulled out of its orbit around the sun to circle the Earth. Some scientists once believed that the moon had been a part of the Earth and became separated during the Earth's formation by our planet's rapid rotation. They thought that the hole left by the moon was the bed of the Pacific Ocean, which was later filled with

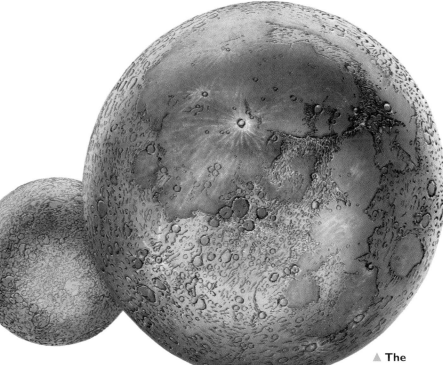

water. This theory was proved to be incorrect after examination of moon rocks brought back by astronauts. Moon rocks have large amounts of minerals that are rare on the Earth, indicating that the moon was probably never a part of the Earth.

▲ The earth-turned face of the moon (top) has many flat plains. The far side (behind) is totally covered by craters.

Orbit of the Moon

The moon revolves around the Earth in a slightly *elliptical* (football-shaped) orbit. Its distance from the Earth varies, averaging about 239,000 miles (384,620 km). One revolution of the moon around the Earth takes about 27 days. This is its *sidereal period*. Because the Earth revolves around the sun, it takes about 29 days for the moon to revolve and return to a position directly between the Earth and the sun—its *synodic period*. One revolution of the moon is about one Earth month.

The moon completes one revolution around the Earth in the same period of time it takes to complete one rotation about its own axis. As a result, about half of the moon's surface is never turned toward the Earth. This unseen surface has often

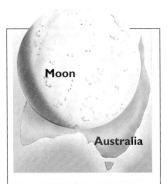

The moon has a diameter of 2,160 miles (3,476 km), which is roughly as wide as Australia. It is 238,000 miles (384,400 km) from the Earth and one "moon day" lasts 29.5 Earth days. The moon has no atmosphere, and the temperature can be as hot as 212°F (100°C) or as cold as -274°F (-170°C).

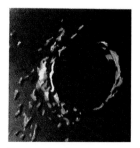
Sun on horizon:
Crater is dark pit.

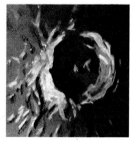
Sun low in sky:
Shadow seen.

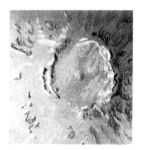
Sun overhead:
Detail is lost.

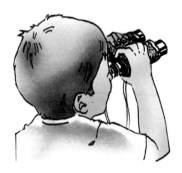

▲ **When the moon is full, the sun is directly overhead, which means that no shadows are cast by crater walls or mountains. This makes them difficult to spot. Craters and other lunar features are best seen when the sun is shining near the moon's horizon, casting long shadows. Then, a simple pair of binoculars will pick up craters, mountains, and the famous "seas."**

been called "the dark side of the moon." But all sides of the moon get sunlight for two weeks each month. Recent photographs taken from manned and unmanned spacecraft circling the moon have given scientists information about this dark side. The surface of the dark side is slightly different from the visible side. It has fewer of the big flat areas called *maria*. Maria means seas, and these flat areas were so named because early astronomers thought they were seas.

Surface of the Moon

The Earth's moon is almost perfectly round and about one-fourth the size of the Earth. Its surface is covered with thousands of deep, wide pits, or *craters*, which may be up to 300 miles (480 km) across. There are often tall mountain peaks in the centers of the craters. Scientists have different opinions about the origin of these craters. Some believe that they were formed by meteors crashing

into the moon. Others believe that the peaks were once explosive volcanoes. When the volcanoes erupted, the explosions hollowed out the areas around them, forming the craters. Other areas, including the maria, are fairly flat.

GRAVITY AND TEMPERATURE. The moon has no *atmosphere* (air or other gas surrounding a celestial body). The gravity on the moon's surface is too weak to prevent the escape of gases into space. The moon's gravitational pull is only one-sixth that of the Earth's. A person who weighs 200 pounds (90 kg) on Earth would only weigh about 33 pounds (15 kg) on the moon!

The temperature on the moon varies greatly. It might be 300°F

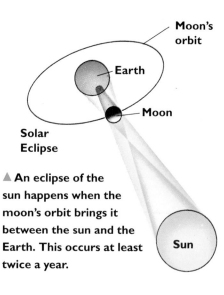

▲ **An eclipse of the sun happens when the moon's orbit brings it between the sun and the Earth. This occurs at least twice a year.**

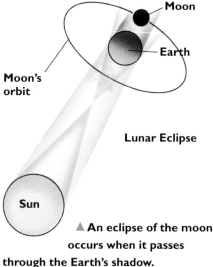

▲ **An eclipse of the moon occurs when it passes through the Earth's shadow.**

LEARN BY DOING

Here is a way to see how gravity works. Tie a length of string to a small plastic bucket. Make sure your knots are strong and you have plenty of room around you. Whirl the bucket around. You'll feel a force tugging it outward—only the string stops the bucket from flying off. The Earth's gravity is like the piece of string holding the moon in its orbit.

▶ During a total eclipse of the sun, only a colored circle flares around it. The moon blocks out the sun almost completely, and for a few minutes the day practically becomes the night. In ancient days, a solar eclipse was viewed with great fear. It was seen as a sign that the gods were displeased.

Solar Eclipse

An eclipse once halted a battle between the armies of ancient Lydia and Medea in 585 B.C. The soldiers were terrified of the sudden darkness.

(150°C) during the "lunar day" (when the sun's rays light the surface) and -180°F (-118°C) at "lunar night" (when the surface is in darkness). Two factors cause these wide differences in temperature: When the sun's rays hit the moon, there is no atmospheric blanket to absorb much of the heat before it reaches the surface, which causes the lunar day to be extremely hot. But the surface material of the moon does not hold in most of the daylight heat, causing the moon to be extremely cold when it is in darkness.

Phases of the Moon

The moon gives off no light of its own. It simply reflects the light from the sun. Only the section reflecting the sun's light can be seen from the Earth. The positions of the Earth, sun, and moon, as the Earth orbits the sun and the moon orbits the Earth, affect the amount of light reflected by the moon, which changes its appearance during each month. These changes in appearance are the *phases* of the moon.

There are four main phases of the moon. When the moon is between the Earth and the sun, and the moon's face is completely shadowed, it is called the *new moon*. Just before and just after the new moon, a thin *crescent* (C-shaped) moon appears. After the new moon, the crescent appears on the eastern side of the moon. Each night, the crescent gets a little larger.

When the entire eastern half of the moon is visible, the moon is in its *first quarter*. When the entire face is lit, the phase is called the *full moon*. The moon is in its *last quarter* when only the entire western half is lit.

Modern-day science has proved that ancient people were not completely wrong in their belief that the moon has tremendous influence on human beings, on some biological processes, and on the planet Earth.

The moon's greatest influence is on

▼ Half of the moon is always in sunlight. The phases of the moon depend on how much of the lit half we can see from the Earth. At the new moon, when the earth, moon, and sun are roughly in line, we cannot see any of the lit half. At the first quarter, we can see half of the part of the moon that is in sunlight, and at full moon we can see it all.

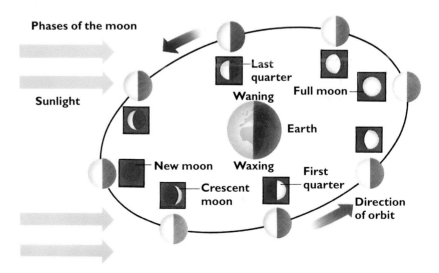

Phases of the moon

Sunlight

Last quarter
Full moon
Waning
Earth
New moon
Waxing
First quarter
Crescent moon
Direction of orbit

Because there is no wind on the moon nor any kind of erosion, this footprint left in the moon- dust by one of the Apollo astronauts will remain undisturbed forever.

◀ Edwin Aldrin, the second man on the moon, photographed by the first: Neil Armstrong. This historic event took place on July 20, 1969. Armstrong and the lunar module *Eagle* are reflected in Aldrin's visor.

MORE, SIR THOMAS (1478–1535)

Sir Thomas More was an English statesman and lawyer. He was also the author of a book called *Utopia*. Utopia was the name he gave to an imaginary island in the middle of the ocean. There was no crime in Utopia, and there were no poor or hungry people. Everyone was equal and worked at the job he or she did best. The happy island of Utopia was very different from the court of King Henry VIII, where More served as lord chancellor (chief minister) of England. He was the most important person in the kingdom, next to the king.

▶ Tests on green moon rock revealed an age of roughly 4.6 thousand million years.

tides. The gravitational pull of the moon causes the tides to rise and fall all over the Earth. There seems no limit to the knowledge that people may receive about the universe from exploring this "new frontier"—the moon.

▶▶▶▶ **FIND OUT MORE** ◀◀◀◀
Aldrin, Edwin; Armstrong, Neil; Astronomy; Earth History; Eclipse; Meteor; Satellite; Solar System; Space Research; Space Travel; Telescope; Tide; Universe

▲ An illustration based on the original *frontispiece* (illustration facing the title page) of Sir Thomas More's *Utopia*. The book described a mythical island where everyone shared in the running of it.

While More was lord chancellor, King Henry decided to divorce his wife, Catherine of Aragon, and marry a lady of the court, Anne Boleyn. Pope Clement VII forbade the divorce, because it was against the laws of the Roman Catholic Church. More did not support King Henry's plan of divorce and, claiming ill health, resigned as lord chancellor.

Later, More refused to sign King Henry's Oath of Supremacy, which stated that the king, not the pope, was the leader of the Church of England. More was imprisoned in the Tower of London. He was convicted of high treason and beheaded on July 6, 1535. In 1935, Pope Pius XI declared More a saint.

▶▶▶▶ **FIND OUT MORE** ◀◀◀◀
English History;
Henry, Kings of England

MORGAN, SIR HENRY

SEE PIRATES AND
PRIVATEERS

MORMON

The people who belong to the Church of Jesus Christ of Latter-day Saints are usually called *Mormons.* Joseph Smith founded the church in

◀ **Thomas More, English statesman, writer, and saint who was executed because of his deep religious convictions.**

1830. Smith claimed he had a *revelation*, or vision, in which God told him to start a new faith. In another vision, Smith said, an angel showed him where to find a set of golden plates, or tablets, with Egyptian writ-

ing on them. These, he said, he translated. His translation has come to be known as *The Book of Mormon— Another Testament of Jesus Christ.* Mormons consider the writings to be holy scripture along with the Bible.

The new religion grew, and Smith

Thomas More named his book *Utopia* from two Greek words, *ou* and *topos*, which mean "not" and "place," or nowhere. Today, when people use the word utopia, they mean a place or situation where everything is impossibly ideal.

◀ **The Church of Jesus Christ of Latter-day Saints (or Mormon Church) was founded by Joseph Smith in 1830 after he received a message from God.**

▼ **The Mormons were not always accepted by other people as they looked for a place to settle and start a new life. They required freedom to worship according to their beliefs.**

▲ The Mormon Tabernacle (famous for its choir) and Mormon office building in Salt Lake City.

▼ Women in a market in Morocco display their produce for sale. For many Muslim women, modesty dictates that they dress to cover themselves completely.

moved his followers to Kirtland, Ohio. Many people in Kirtland did not want the Mormons to live there, and forced them to move away. They went to Missouri and then to Illinois, where they founded the city of Nauvoo. After a few years there, Joseph Smith was killed by an angry mob. Brigham Young became the new leader, and the Mormons moved to the Great Salt Lake valley in Utah. Today, there are more than 6 million members of the church worldwide; about one million live in Utah.

▶▶▶▶ FIND OUT MORE ◀◀◀◀
Smith, Joseph; Utah; Young, Brigham

🏴 MOROCCO

Morocco has the broadest plains and the tallest mountains in North Africa. It lies on the northwest coast of Africa. The port of Tangier is on the Strait of Gibraltar, the narrow channel between the Atlantic Ocean and the Mediterranean Sea. Morocco's west coast is on the Atlantic, and on the north it borders the Mediterranean. It is bounded on the east and southeast by Algeria and on the south by the Western Sahara.

The rugged Atlas Mountains rise to a height of more than 13,000 feet (3,900 m) in Morocco. An area of highlands called Er Rif parallels the Mediterranean coast. Most Moroccans live in the Atlantic coastal plain, where rainfall provides a water supply. Located there are Rabat, the capital, and Casablanca, the largest city and main seaport. Two historic cities are found inland near the mountains: Fez, containing a Muslim university more than 1,000 years old, and Marrakesh, famous for its leather goods.

Farming is the mainstay of the Moroccan economy, although less than 20 percent of Morocco can be cultivated. Wheat and barley are the leading crops. Corn, beans, peas, and grapes are also grown. Orange, lemon, and almond trees and date palms grow well in the warm climate. Phosphates are mined and exported. Other minerals are ores of iron, manganese, zinc, lead, and cobalt and anthracite coal. Cork oak, evergreen oak, juniper, cedar, fir, and pine grow in the millions of acres of forest.

Morocco's chief industries include food processing; leather tanning; and the manufacture of textiles, chemicals, and cement. Hydroelectric plants supply the country's power.

Bedouin Arabs make up the majority of the population in Morocco. The Berbers, who at one time ruled most of northwest Africa, live in isolated villages in the high mountain areas.

The first known foreign invaders were the Phoenicians who established trading posts on the Mediterranean coast in the 1100s B.C. Carthage and then Rome conquered the area. After a period of Vandal and Byzantine Christian rule, the Arabs conquered Morocco in A.D. 682, when they invaded the region to spread the religion of Islam. In 1212, the large Muslim empire fell to Spain.

In 1415, Portugal captured Moroccan ports, but the Moors (Spanish Muslims) later defeated Portugal. Germany, France, and Spain became rivals over control of Morocco. In 1904, Morocco was divided into French and Spanish protectorates. France and Spain recognized Moroccan independence in 1956.

region. But many Saharans support a group called the Polisario Front, which opposes Moroccan rule. Fighting between Morocco and the Polisario Front continued into the late 1980s. A truce was reached in 1990, pending a referendum.

▶▶▶▶ **FIND OUT MORE** ◀◀◀◀
Africa; Byzantine Empire;
Mediterranean Sea

ATLANTIC
OCEAN

0   150   300 Miles
0   150   300   450 Kilometers
© 1994 GeoSystems, an R.R. Donnelley & Sons Company

Morocco is a constitutional monarchy with a *unicameral* (single chamber) legislature and a king as head of state. Since 1979, Morocco has occupied the Western Sahara

MOROCCO

Capital city
Rabat
(519,000 people)

Area
172,414 square miles
(446,518 sq. km)

Population
25,228,000 people

Government
Constitutional monarchy

Natural resources
Phosphates, iron ore,
manganese, lead, zinc

Export products
Food and beverages,
semiprocessed foods,
consumer goods,
phosphates

Unit of money
Dirham

Official language
Arabic

MORSE, SAMUEL F. B. (1791–1872)

Samuel Finley Breese Morse was an American inventor and artist. He designed the first telegraph powerful enough to send signals over long distances. To make it possible for messages to be sent over the telegraph, Morse invented the system later known as "Morse code."

Samuel Morse was born in Charleston, Massachusetts. As a young man, he wanted to be an artist. He studied art at Yale University and at the Royal Academy of Arts in London, England. When

Casablanca, the biggest town in Morocco, has many white buildings in it. The name *casa blanca* means "white house" in Spanish. The town grew up around a small Arab village, now called the Old Medina.

▲ Samuel F. B. Morse, American artist and inventor of the telegraph.

▼ A diagram of Morse's electric telegraph system (1882). From the 1770s on, there were many experiments with telegraph systems. But Morse invented a code to translate messages over the wires that was simple to use, and so his method was adopted.

Morse returned from London, his greatest ambition was to paint large historical paintings for the United States Capitol, then being built in Washington, D.C. He traveled to Europe again to prepare for the possibility of working on the Capitol. When Morse was returning to the U.S. from Europe in 1832, he met a man who talked about the possibility of sending a signal over an electric wire. Morse became very interested in this invention.

When he did not receive a commission to paint the Capitol paintings, he began to experiment with electrical machines. He believed that electricity could be used to send messages over wires for long distances. He worked on this project for ten years, living close to poverty. He taught art to pay for his research.

Morse's first attempt to make a long-distance system ended in disaster. He stretched a wire from Manhattan across New York Harbor to Governors Island. But a ship's anchor broke the wire, and the people who had come to see the demonstration left angrily.

In 1843, Congress finally gave Morse the money he needed to test the telegraph. He set up a telegraph wire from Washington, D.C. to Baltimore, Maryland. While members of Congress watched, he sent the Morse code message, "What hath God wrought?" It was received 50 miles (80 km) away. Morse became an immediate success. Telegraph companies were soon set up in the United States and Europe.

▶▶▶▶ **FIND OUT MORE** ◀◀◀◀
Communication; Morse Code;
Telegraph

MORSE CODE

The Morse code is a system of dots and dashes used to send messages by telegraph wire. The code was named after its inventor, Samuel F. B. Morse. You can see the code set out on this page below.

Morse code was an important way to send messages before the telephone was invented. Most telegrams are now sent by a machine called a *teletype*, which converts a special code directly into printed letters.

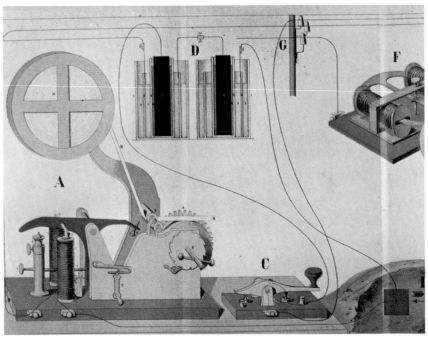

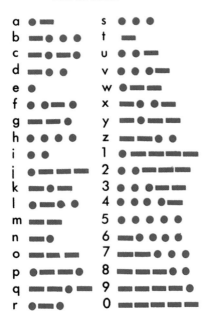

Morse Code

▲ The dots and dashes of the Morse code. An SOS signal is three dots and three dashes followed by three dots.

Much information is sent also by an automatic facsimile (fax).

The dots and dashes of the Morse code are based on timing. The dot is a rapid click. A dash sounds twice as long as a dot. Each letter of the alphabet is represented by a different combination of dots and dashes. The code also includes numerals and punctuation marks. A space between words is as long as six dots. The telegraph operator taps out the message by pressing and releasing a special telegraph key. When he or she presses down the key, an electrical *impulse,* or signal, is sent over the telegraph wire. At the other end, an instrument called a *receiver* registers the length of each impulse by a buzzing sound—short for a dot and long for a dash. Messages in Morse code are also sent over radio waves. Guglielmo Marconi (1874–1937) was the Italian scientist who invented a system for sending Morse code messages long distances without wires.

▶▶▶▶ **FIND OUT MORE** ◀◀◀◀

Morse, Samuel F. B.; Radio; Signal; Telecommunications; Telegraph

MOSAIC

For more than 2,000 years, people have created mosaics to decorate the walls, floors, and ceilings of buildings. Mosaics are designs made by fitting together small pieces of hard, colored material. The small pieces are called *tesserae.* Tesserae can be any shape. Marble, glass, tile, pebbles, shells, and even seeds are used as tesserae. Marble and tile are usually used for floor mosaics. Glass and the more breakable materials are used for mosaics on walls, ceilings, tabletops, and other surfaces.

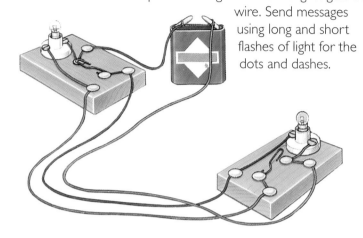

LEARN BY DOING

You can make your own Morse transmitter using flashing lights. Make a pair of switches using thumbtacks and paper clips, as shown. Connect the switches to a battery and lamp holders and connect the two lamp holders together with long lengths of wire. Send messages using long and short flashes of light for the dots and dashes.

The ancient Egyptians made brightly colored mosaics showing plants and animals. The ancient Greeks, and even more so the Romans, created very complicated floor mosaics using marble tesserae. Many mosaics were discovered in the Roman city of Pompeii. The city was covered over by volcanic lava from the eruption of Mount Vesuvius in about A.D. 79. The Pompeiian mosaic on the next page shows four musicians. Look closely, and you can see how the artist used lighter and darker tesserae to make shading for the shadows on the floor and wall, the folds of the garments, and the roundness of the body parts. The mosaic is almost like a painting.

During the Byzantine period in art (A.D. 330–1453), mosaics became one of the most widely used decorations in churches and cathedrals. The Byzantine artists used glass tesserae. Glass is shinier than marble,

The world's largest mosaic adorns four walls in the National University, in Mexico City. It shows historical scenes. The two largest mosaic-covered walls are 13,000 square feet (1,200 sq. m) in area.

◀ This mosaic is from the front entrance of a house in Pompeii. The words *CAVE CANEM* mean "Beware of the Dog." This did not always mean that there was a guard dog inside, but it did mean that passersby were not welcome within.

▲ A mosaic in the church of Santa Prassede in Rome, Italy, shows the Virgin Mary and Jesus. It is one of the best examples of Byzantine art in Rome.

▲ The finest houses in Pompeii were decorated with marble mosaics. Some of the mosaics had a light and humorous theme, such as this one of a group of dancing musicians.

▼ Mosaic makers had apprentices to cut up the stone for them. Sometimes the central picture or design would be created in the workshop, then taken to the house to be put in place.

and light reflects from it. So the tesserae seem to glitter.

Compare the Byzantine mosaic of Christ and the Virgin Mary with the Roman mosaic of the musicians. You can see that the colors of the Byzantine mosaic are sharp and bright, while the Roman colors are soft. The Byzantine mosaic contains a great deal of gold, but the Roman mosaic has none. With marble tesserae, the artist can use only the natural colors of marble. There is no gold marble, but glass can be tinted with gold or any color the artist chooses. Byzantine artists used a lot of gold in their religious mosaics. That color seemed to give a feeling of the greatness of God.

The human figures in Byzantine mosaics are stiffer than in Roman

mosaics. The Byzantine artists did not try to make their religious figures look realistic. The artists wanted them to look like people from heaven—different from ordinary human beings. Look closely at the tesserae in the clothing of the Byzantine figures. You can see that the pieces of glass are like a design. The colors are arranged in stripes that move in various directions. The draped clothing of the Virgin Mary, as well as the main facial features, are outlined in a darker color. Outlining makes the figures look stiffer than those in the Roman mosaic, where no outlining is used. The

Roman figures are natural looking.

In Central and South America, Inca, Aztec, and Maya artists created designs in stone mosaics to decorate their places of worship. Artists in Persia and India created beautiful glass and tile mosaics. The doorways, domes, and minarets of some Persian mosques are covered entirely with tile mosaics. These mosaics are mostly blue, with green, yellow, and orange plantlike decorations and quotations from the Koran, the holy book of Islam containing the sayings of Muhammad.

▶ ▶ ▶ ▶ **FIND OUT MORE** ◀ ◀ ◀ ◀
Byzantine Empire; Pompeii; Romanesque Art

MOSCOW

Moscow is the capital city of Russia. From 1917 to 1991, it was also the capital and largest city of the former Union of Soviet Socialist Republics (U.S.S.R.) About 9 million people live in Moscow.

Although Moscow lies far inland, it is sometimes referred to as the "Port of Five Seas." Ships from the Baltic, White, Black, and Caspian seas and the Sea of Azov travel to Moscow by way of the Volga-Don and Moscow canals and the Moskva River.

Moscow streets are laid out in rings and semicircles. The *Kremlin* is in the center of the city. The Kremlin Palace is surrounded by a high stone wall. In front of it is Red Square, where parades were held. Facing on the square are the tomb of Vladimir Lenin (founder of the Soviet state) and the famous Cathedral of St. Basil.

Moscow has many theaters, a large university, a library, museums, art galleries, a stadium for sporting events, and many parks.

Moscow is also a manufacturing city. Steel, tools, chemicals, cars, air-

LEARN BY DOING

You can make your own mosaic using pebbles, seeds, shells, and bits of broken china as tesserae. You will need a square of very stiff cardboard and some strong glue. Draw your design with colors on the board. Begin by gluing the tesserae along the edges first, working inward. When the glue dries, your mosaic is ready.

planes, furniture, textiles, and many other articles are made there.

The city was founded as a fortified village in the 1100s. Grand Duke Ivan III made Moscow a political capital during his reign (1462–1505). The seat of government was moved to St. Petersburg in 1712.

French troops under Napoleon occupied Moscow in 1812, but soon afterward, a fire, believed to have been set by the Russians, burned most of the city to the ground. The French, defeated by hunger and cold, retreated from Russia. Moscow was the site of bloody revolutions against the czar in 1905 and 1917. In 1917, the capital was moved back from St. Petersburg, the old czarist capital, to the new Soviet capital of Moscow.

In 1991, many changes occurred in the U.S.S.R. Several Soviet states, including Russia itself, strove for independence. For some it was granted. Moscow is, therefore, no longer such a center of power. Russia and several other former Soviet states now form a community—the Commonwealth of Independent States (CIS).

▶ ▶ ▶ ▶ **FIND OUT MORE** ◀ ◀ ◀ ◀
Kremlin; Russian History; Russia

▲ **St. Basil's Cathedral, with its many splendid domes, is in one of the most historic parts of Moscow, near the Kremlin.**

The famous Red Square in Moscow did not get its name from the Russian Revolution or the Soviet flag. Its name came from the Russian word *krasnya*, which means both "red" and "beautiful." The square has had its name since the Middle Ages.

▲ **The brightly colored dome of a mosque at Samarra in Iraq. Many hours of painstaking decoration have gone into making this place of worship worthy of the God of Islam.**

MOSQUE

A mosque is a house of worship for Muslims, people who believe in the religion of Islam. A mosque can be small and simple, but some are magnificent examples of architecture. Most are beautiful, domed buildings, supported by graceful pillars.

Every mosque has certain basic parts. At the entrance is an open courtyard with a fountain or pool, in which people wash themselves before praying. Worshipers pray in a closed meeting room called a *musalla*. Men and women are separated and pray in different parts of the musalla. All face an ornamental niche (set-in space) called a *mihrab*. This points the way to Islam's holy city, Mecca. Muslims always pray facing in the direction of Mecca because Muhammad, the chief prophet of the faith of Islam, was born in that city. When Muslims pray, they kneel and bend their heads to the ground and finally lie prostrate, or flat, on the ground. The Koran, the holy book of Islam, is read in the mosque from a pulpit, or

▼ **Part of the mosque at Isfahan built by Abbas the Great. It is highly decorated with patterns based on geometric designs and plant shapes.**

platform, called the *mimbar*. High above at least one corner of the mosque is a *minaret* or tower. A man called a *muezzin* climbs up in the tower five times a day to call the faithful to prayer. A religious school may be part of the mosque.

▶▶▶▶ **FIND OUT MORE** ◀◀◀◀
Islam; Muhammad

MOSQUITO

The common name for any of about 2,500 kinds of two-winged flies is mosquito. The mosquito has a narrow body and long, slender wings. The mouthparts of a mosquito form a hollow, tubelike organ called a *proboscis*, which is not much wider than a hair. The male mosquito uses the proboscis like a straw to feed on plant fluids. Female mosquitoes feed on blood. The proboscis of a female mosquito can pierce the skin of animals.

When a female mosquito bites, it pushes the proboscis into the victim's skin, probing for a capillary (tiny blood vessel). While biting, the mosquito injects some saliva into the wound. The saliva prevents the blood from clotting and clogging the proboscis. The saliva is what causes the swelling and itching of a mosquito bite.

If a mosquito bites a human being or other animal suffering from a certain disease, the mosquito often carries off such disease germs in its saliva. It injects them into the blood of its next victim. In this way, a mosquito may carry such diseases as malaria and yellow fever, often infecting great numbers of people. Fortunately, not all mosquitoes are disease carriers. The common house mosquito is not a carrier of disease.

Female mosquitoes lay their eggs in swamps, marshes, lagoons, and other pools of quiet water. They may lay them in a rain barrel. The larvae are called *wrigglers*, because of their

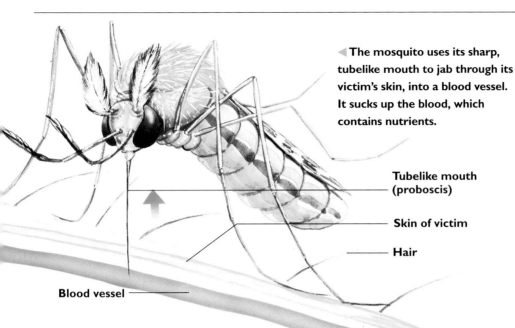

◄ The mosquito uses its sharp, tubelike mouth to jab through its victim's skin, into a blood vessel. It sucks up the blood, which contains nutrients.

Female mosquitoes live up to 30 days. Males only live for between 7 and 10 days.

Tubelike mouth (proboscis)

Skin of victim

Hair

Blood vessel

wriggling motion in the water. The pupae are *bullheads*.

People have found that the best way to get rid of mosquitoes is to destroy them while they are in the larva stage. This can be done by pouring a thin layer of oil over the water in which they are growing. The oil prevents air from reaching the larvae, causing them to suffocate. Airplanes have sometimes been used to spray insecticides and other chemicals over bodies of water in regions infested with disease-carrying mosquitoes. If possible, it is best to prevent mosquitoes from breeding at all. This can be done by draining swamps, filling in mud holes, and covering or destroying any containers that can hold water. Rain barrels, for example, are potential breeding places for mosquitoes and should be covered.

▶ ▶ ▶ ▶ **FIND OUT MORE** ◄ ◄ ◄ ◄
Disease; Fly; Insect

MOSSES AND LIVERWORTS

Mosses and liverworts are tiny plants that usually live in damp, shady places. They make up the plant group called *Bryophyta*. Mosses and liverworts were two of the first kinds of plants to live on

land. Scientists have found traces of these plants. Some are 350 million years old.

Mosses and liverworts grow on soil, rocks, tree bark, and in shallow water. They are hardy plants that live on all the continents of the world. Mosses and liverworts do not have true roots. Instead, they have threadlike growths called *rhizoids*. Rhizoids do two important things that roots do. They absorb water and hold the plant in place. Neither mosses nor liverworts have flowers.

Mosses are small—rarely more than 1.5 inches (4 cm) long. Many of them are *evergreen*, growing in both cold and warm weather. The tiny moss plants grow

Swan-necked tread moss

Racomitrium lanuginosum

▲ The swan-necked thread moss is a common woodland moss. The *Racomitrium* grows on mountains and tundra.

PARTS OF A MOSS

Spore pod capsule

Stalk

Simple leaves

◄ Mosses send out stalks with a pod at the tip. The pod releases thousands of spores to form new plants.

Silky wall feather moss

Leucobryum glaucum

▲ The silky wall feather moss is easily recognized by the yellow tips of its main shoots. The *Leucobryum glaucum* forms cushions that are useful to flower arrangers.

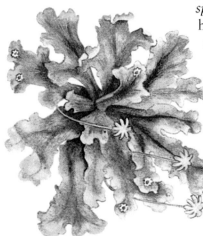

Marchantia polymorpha

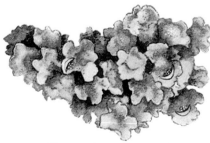

Crescent-cup liverwort

▲ The *marchantia polymorpha* is a liverwort found on wet paths, river banks, and greenhouses. It has goblet-shaped gemma cups from which reproductive tissue is scattered. The crescent-cup liverwort, also found in damp places, is named for the shape of its gemma cups.

very closely together, forming carpets or pads.

A moss plant reproduces in two stages—*sexual* and *asexual*. The sexual stage involves the joining of male and female sex cells. Some adult plants have capsules containing *sperm*, or male sex cells. Other plants have *eggs*, or female sex cells. When the sperm capsules ripen and burst open, sperm cells are carried (usually by drops of rain or dew) to egg cells. The sperm unites with, or *fertilizes*, the egg. Then the asexual stage begins. The fertilized egg grows into a stalk with a spore capsule at the end. When the capsule ripens, it bursts open and scatters its spores. These spores grow into new male and female plants.

Mosses are useful in nature because they are among the first plants to grow in barren areas. Their decaying remains form soil in which other plants can grow. *Sphagnum* moss is used as a moisture-holding cover for soil in gardens. It is also sterilized and used in absorbent surgical dressings. Decaying sphagnum forms *peat*, a kind of fuel.

Each liverwort plant looks like a tiny leaf. The main body of the plant, the *thallus*, is shaped somewhat like a human liver. This is why the plant is called a liverwort. People once mistakenly believed that liverworts cured liver diseases. Liverworts, like mosses, reproduce in two stages.

▶ ▶ ▶ ▶ **FIND OUT MORE** ◀ ◀ ◀ ◀
Club Moss; Lichen; Plant; Plant Distribution; Plant Kingdom; Plants of the Past; Reproduction

MOTELS

SEE HOTELS AND MOTELS

MOTHER GOOSE

SEE NURSERY RHYME; PERRAULT, CHARLES

MOTHS

SEE BUTTERFLIES AND MOTHS

☼ MOTION

You watch objects in motion all the time. Tree branches wave in the wind. While you and your friends walk home from school, cars speed past you, and high overhead a jet plane zooms across the sky. Furthermore, while all this is going on, the moon is circling the Earth, and the Earth and the other planets are circling the sun.

Nearly all motion—whether the motion is a river flowing or the Earth's movement around the sun—is described by three scientific laws. These laws of motion were discovered by Sir Isaac Newton about 300 years ago.

Newton's first law says that an object at rest tends to stay at rest; an object in motion tends to stay in motion. The tendency all objects have to keep moving—or not to move if they are at rest—is called *inertia*. To make an object move you must push or pull it. A scientist would say you exerted force on it. Once the object is moving, and if no other forces acted on it, it would move forever. But on Earth, another force does act on objects. This force is called *friction*. Friction occurs whenever a moving object touches another object. If you rub your hands together, the heat you feel is caused by friction. Friction slows down movement and stops things moving. When the brakes are applied, the friction between an automobile's wheels and the ground stops the automobile.

Newton's second law explains the changes in motion that force can cause. When a new force is applied to a moving object, what happens depends on two things—the weight of the object and the size of the force.

To measure the speed of a moving object, scientists use *velocity*—how much distance an object moves in a certain amount of time. A turtle's velocity may be 4 inches (10 cm) a minute. A rocket's velocity may be 18,000 miles (29,000 km) an hour.

When a force is applied to an object, the object accelerates. *Acceleration* is the measurement of how quickly and how much velocity changes. When one of your parents steps on the gas pedal in the car, you feel the car accelerating (moving faster and faster).

Newton's third law says that for every action, there is an equal but

opposite reaction. One example of this is the lawn sprinkler with spinning arms. As the water squirts, the arms turn in the opposite direction.

▶ ▶ ▶ ▶ **FIND OUT MORE** ◀ ◀ ◀ ◀
Energy; Friction; Jet Propulsion; Newton, Sir Isaac; Perpetual Motion; Rocket

▲ **To put a motorcycle in motion requires force, supplied by the engine. The capacity of the engine and the weight of the machine and its rider determine the speed at which the motorcycle will go.**

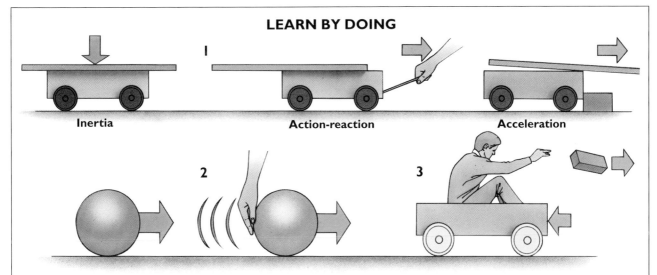

LEARN BY DOING

Inertia

Action-reaction

Acceleration

1. Place a board on a wagon and give the wagon a hard jerk forward. The wagon will move forward, leaving the resting board *at rest*. Push the wagon and board so both are in motion. When the wagon stops, the board continues.

2. Roll a ball across the floor. Try giving it a hard push. Try pushing a Ping-Pong ball and a softball with the same force. What happens? Pushing gives acceleration. The heavier the object, the smaller the acceleration.

3. Take a few bricks and sit in a wagon. Throw each brick out as hard as you can. Make sure no one else is nearby. The wagon rolls backward when the object is thrown forward, proving that for every action there is an equal opposite reaction.

MOTION PICTURE

Motion pictures of one kind or another probably play a big part in your education and entertainment. Perhaps you help your family make home movies. At school you very likely see educational films about history, science, or arithmetic. Many motion pictures are shown on television. You probably even go to a movie theater now and then.

The picture you see on the screen seems to be moving. But you are really seeing a series of pictures flashing one after another, very rapidly. When a motion picture camera is running, the film keeps moving and stopping. Each time it stops, the shutter opens briefly and a picture is taken. This happens 24 times a second while the camera is going. Look at 24 pictures on a strip of movie film, or one second's worth. You have to look at a hundred frames to see much difference in the pictures. The film is then projected on a screen at the rate of 24 pictures a second, the same speed at which it was photographed. At this speed, the human eye sees only a continuously moving picture.

How Motion Pictures Are Made

Thousands of people are needed to make a big feature movie—the kind shown at movie theaters and later on television. But even a simple movie requires the teamwork of a number of people. A writer produces the *script*, or story line, of a movie. Sometimes the writer adapts the script from a play or novel. The *producer* selects the script and is in charge of the money. He or she also hires the *director*. Together, the producer and the director select the *cast*, the actors and actresses who will appear in the film. The director tells the cast what to do and the camera people when to start and stop their cameras. *Set designers* build any settings or background buildings needed for the movie. They also arrange *props*, the furniture and other objects used in the movie. *Costume designers* design and make clothing for the cast to wear in the film. The *makeup* crew apply cos-

▲ Movie and television films are made out of lots of separate scenes. Each scene may involve several "takes," which are marked off on a clapperboard to keep them in order.

▶ *Cinematic* (movie) film is wound onto a reel in a lightproof cartridge or magazine. The holes in the sides of the film fit over teeth on drive sprockets in the camera, which pull the roll of film past the film gate. This is where light is directed onto the film more than 24 times each second. Each exposure records the scene as a separate picture. The film has three light-sensitive layers, and each layer reacts to light of a certain color.

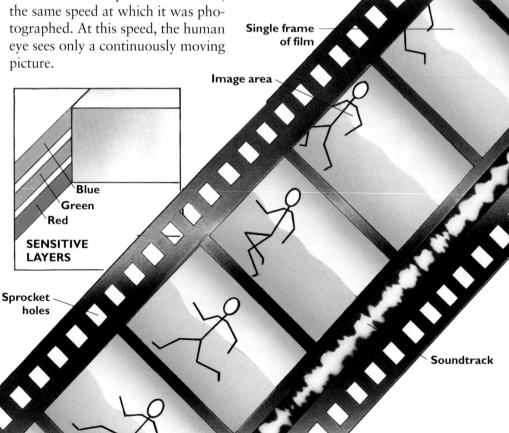

Blue
Green
Red
SENSITIVE LAYERS

Single frame of film

Image area

Sprocket holes

Soundtrack

metics. Sometimes a *composer* writes music to go with the film, and an orchestra plays the music. *Sound recordists* record the music and all sounds made in the film. They also make sure that the sound is clear and accurate.

All this work is performed in a motion picture *studio,* or on *location,* when pictures are filmed in a natural setting. A movie about a mountain climber, for instance, might be filmed in the Rocky Mountains in Wyoming.

A motion picture is not filmed from beginning to end without stopping. Little scenes are shot separately. It may take several weeks or months and many scenes to film a picture. After all the filming is finished, the *film editor* arranges the hundreds of feet of film taken by the camera people into a smooth-flowing film. The director usually supervises the editing to make sure that the film is put together as he or she wants it.

Early Days of Motion Pictures
People began inventing simple devices to make moving pictures in the 1800s. An American named Coleman Sellers invented the *kinematoscope* in 1861. This consisted of a series of pictures mounted on a wheel. The wheel was spun around, and the pictures seemed to move. In 1878, a British photographer named Eadweard Muybridge set up 24 cameras at a racetrack. Strings were stretched across the track to the cameras. When a horse raced by, breaking the strings, the cameras recorded the motion of the running horse. The American inventor, Thomas Edison, developed a viewing machine called the *kinetoscope* in 1891. A person who looked through a peephole in

▶ **When editing a film, individual frames are chosen to follow each other. The frames are cut up and glued (spliced) together in the new sequence.**

LEARN BY DOING

You need four sheets of poster board. Draw a person without arms. Trace this picture onto the other three cards. Draw in the arms on each as shown. Fold each card down the center. Place the outstretched arm pictures between the other two. Glue the pictures to a knitting needle and spin it. What happens?

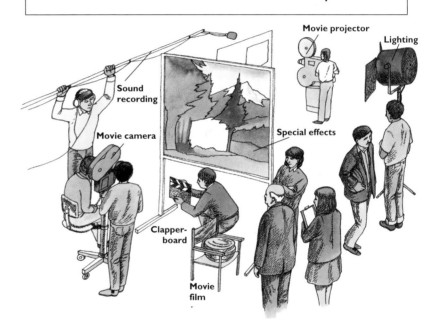

▲ **A film set. The camera is filming a fake background projected onto a screen by a movie projector.**

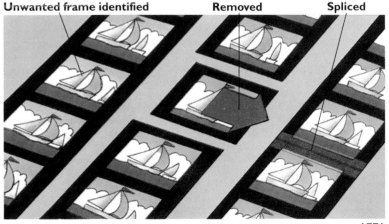

Unwanted frame identified   Removed   Spliced

▲ **Clark Gable and Vivien Leigh in *Gone With the Wind*, the 1939 blockbuster that used Technicolor successfully.**

The largest cinema in the world is the Radio City Music Hall, New York City, which has the vast total of 5,874 seats.

the kinetoscope saw a short series of pictures. One showed a person sneezing. Another showed waves rolling to shore. Kinetoscope parlors, the forerunners of movie theaters, were built in New York, Paris, and London. They were tremendously popular.

The first American film to tell a story was *The Great Train Robbery*, produced by Edwin S. Porter in 1903.

The first *nickelodeons* also appeared in 1903. They were gaudy theaters that showed short movies for the price of a nickel. Piano players provided the music. They played fast and loudly during exciting scenes, but gently and sweetly during love scenes. One of the first great American directors was D. W. Griffith. He produced *The Birth of a Nation* in 1915. Griffith used this Civil War story to try out new camera techniques, such as the *close-up* shot, to make the audience feel more involved in the film.

The Hollywood Era

As longer feature films began to be made, large movie houses took the place of nickelodeons. Movies became big business. Small, independent producers were replaced by large production companies, such as

Warner Brothers. Many of the large companies established their headquarters in southern California, because its sunny, warm climate was ideal for moviemaking. Hollywood, California, became "the motion picture capital of the world."

Leading actors and actresses became known as *stars*. The success of a movie began to depend on the popularity of the actor or actress who played the starring role. Each star became known for a particular specialty. Mary Pickford, known as "America's Sweetheart," played innocent young girl roles. Tom Mix and his trained horse, Tony, played in western movies. Rudolf Valentino became the leading romantic male star. Charlie Chaplin was the most famous comedian. He played a sad, but always hopeful, tramp. Movies called *serials* became very popular. These were movies made in short chapters. One chapter was shown at a time. Each one ended with the hero in desperate danger, perhaps hanging from a cliff, so that the audience would be sure to come back the following week to see what happened. Serials were sometimes called *cliffhangers*. The *Perils of Pauline* was a favorite.

▼ **Humphrey Bogart and Ingrid Bergman in the 1943 film *Casablanca*.**

▲ Marlon Brando in one of his early starring roles in the film *On the Waterfront,* 1954, which won him an Academy Award for best actor.

European Film Making

Movie making began in Europe at about the same time as in the United States. But during World War I, European filmmakers had to stop production. Hollywood movies became international favorites. After the war, Europeans again began to make their own motion pictures.

The Germans began to make films that explored the human mind. *The Cabinet of Doctor Caligari*, directed by Robert Weine in 1919, was one of these. It was photographed as if seen through the eyes of a person in a mental institution. The Germans also contributed many new technical advances to filmmaking. The French began to make films that were truly individual in style. These films were often intimate studies of lower-class life in France. Filmmaking in the former Soviet Union came under government control. Soviet directors, among them Sergei Eisenstein, began to use film to teach their audiences about Communist ideals. European moviemaking was again interrupted, this time by World War II. But a trend toward making more realistic movies, which had developed in the thirties, continued after the war.

When films made in one country are shown in a country speaking a different language, something has to be done to the films so that the viewers will understand them. For instance, for a film in which French is spoken, a new sound track is made with English-speaking actors speaking the words. This process is called *dubbing*. Another way of making a foreign film understandable is to print an English translation of the words spoken by the actors at the bottom of the screen. The printed words are called *subtitles*.

The Beginning of Sound

When radio programs became popular about 1925, many people stopped attending movies. But in 1927, the first sound film, *The Jazz Singer,* starring Al Jolson, was put out by Warner Brothers. It had only a few lines of dialogue and several songs, but it was an immediate success. The new "talkies" replaced the silent films. Many actors and actresses with foreign accents or unpleasant-sounding voices lost their jobs. Comedians, such as the rowdy Marx Brothers and W. C. Fields, introduced a new type of film humor. Lively movies, called *musicals*, filled with dancing and singing, were made. Fred Astaire and Ginger Rogers were dancing partners in a long list of happy musicals. Shirley Temple, with her dimples and golden curls, became one of the world's best-loved child actresses. Gangster, detective, and horror stories were filmed, too.

In 1933, a way of filming movies in color was perfected. It was called *Technicolor*. One of the biggest and most successful Technicolor films was *Gone With the Wind*, a Civil War drama shot in 1939. The new color process made the film's elaborate costumes and sets seem more real.

QUIZ

1. At how many frames per second are most motion pictures filmed (and shown)?
2. What are *props*?
3. What is known as "the motion picture capital of the world"?
4. What was the first feature-length color cartoon?
5. What are *subtitles*?
6. What are *documentaries*?

(Answers on page 1792)

▼ Before 1900, a few motion pictures used sound, but it was not easy to adjust the sound with the action on screen. In the mid-1920s, a system was developed that linked sound on records to the projector. In 1927, in *The Jazz Singer*, Al Jolson actually spoke a few words. Moviemaking history had been made. The "talkies" had arrived.

Julie Andrews

Marlene Dietrich

Eddie Murphy

Year	Best Picture	Best Actor	Best Actress	Best Director
1927–1928	Wings	Emil Jannings (The Way of All Flesh and The Last Command)	Janet Gaynor (Seventh Heaven, Street Angel and Sunrise)	Frank Borzage (Seventh Heaven) Lewis Milestone (Two Arabian Nights)
1928–1929	The Broadway Melody	Warren Baxter (In Old Arizona)	Mary Pickford (Coquette)	Frank Lloyd (The Divine Lady)
1929–1930	All Quiet on the Western Front	George Arliss (Disraeli)	Norma Shearer (The Divorcee)	Lewis Milestone (All Quiet on the Western Front)
1930–1931	Cimarron	Lionel Barrymore (A Free Soul)	Marie Dressler (Min and Bill)	Norman Taurog (Skippy)
1931–1932	Grand Hotel	Frederic March (Dr. Jekyll and Mr. Hyde) Wallace Beery (The Champ)	Helen Hayes (The Sin of Madelon Claudet)	Frank Borzage (Bad Girl)
1934	It Happened One Night	Clark Gable (It Happened One Night)	Claudette Colbert (It Happened One Night)	Frank Capra (It Happened One Night)
1935	Mutiny on the Bounty	Victor Mclaglen (The Informer)	Bette Davis (Dangerous)	John Ford (The Informer)
1936	The Great Ziegfeld	Paul Muni (The Story of Louis Pasteur)	Luise Rainer (The Great Ziegfeld)	Frank Capra (Mr. Deeds Goes to Town)
1937	The Life of Emile Zola	Spencer Tracy (Captains Courageous)	Luise Rainer (The Good Earth)	Leo Carey (The Awful Truth)
1938	You Can't Take It With You	Spencer Tracy (Boys' Town)	Bette Davis (Jezebel)	Frank Capra (You Can't Take It With You)
1939	Gone With the Wind	Robert Donat (Goodbye Mr. Chips)	Vivien Leigh (Gone With the Wind)	Victor Fleming (Gone With the Wind)
1940	Rebecca	James Stewart (The Philadelphia Story)	Ginger Rogers (Kitty Foyle)	John Ford (The Grapes of Wrath)
1941	How Green Was My Valley	Gary Cooper (Sergeant York)	Joan Fontaine (Suspicion)	John Ford (How Green Was My Valley)
1942	Mrs. Miniver	James Cagney (Yankee Doodle Dandy)	Greer Garson (Mrs. Miniver)	William Wyler (Mrs. Miniver)
1943	Casablanca	Paul Lucas (Watch on the Rhine)	Jennifer Jones (The Song of Bernadette)	Michael Curtiz (Casablanca)
1944	Going My Way	Bing Crosby (Gaslight)	Ingrid Bergman (Going My Way)	Leo Carey (Going My Way)
1945	The Lost Weekend	Ray Milland (The Lost Weekend)	Joan Crawford (Mildred Pierce)	Billy Wilder (The Lost Weekend)
1946	The Best Years of Our Lives	Frederic March (The Best Years of Our Lives)	Olivia de Havilland (To Each His Own)	William Wyler (The Best Years of Our Lives)
1947	Gentleman's Agreement	Ronald Colman (A Double Life)	Loretta Young (The Farmer's Daughter)	Elia Kazan (Gentleman's Agreement)
1948	Hamlet	Laurence Olivier (Hamlet)	Jane Wyman (Johnny Belinda)	John Huston (Treasure of Sierra Madre)
1949	All the King's Men	Broderick Crawford (All The King's men)	Olivia de Havilland (The Heiress)	Joseph L. Mankievicz (A Letter to Three Wives)
1950	All About Eve	José Ferrer (Cyrano de Bergerac)	Judy Holliday (Born Yesterday)	Joseph L.Mankievicz (All About Eve)
1951	An American in Paris	Humphrey Bogart (The African Queen)	Vivien Leigh (A Streetcar Named Desire)	George Stevens (A Place in the Sun)
1952	The Greatest Show on Earth	Gary Cooper (High Noon)	Shirley Booth (Come Back, Little Sheba)	John Ford (The Quiet Man)
1953	From Here to Eternity	William Holden (Stalag 17)	Audrey Hepburn (Roman Holiday)	Fred Zinnemann (From Here to Eternity)
1954	On the Waterfront	Marlon Brando (On the Waterfront)	Grace Kelly (The Country Girl)	Elia Kazan (On the Waterfront)
1955	Marty	Ernest Borgnine (Marty)	Anna Magnani (The Rose Tattoo)	Delbert Mann (Marty)
1956	Around the World in 80 Days	Yul Brynner (The King and I)	Ingrid Bergman (Anastasia)	George Stevens (Giant)
1957	The Bridge on the River Kwai	Alec Guinness (The Bridge the River Kwai)	Joanne Woodward (TheThree Faces of Eve)	David Lean (The Bridge on the River Kwai)
1958	Gigi	David Niven (Separate Tables)	Susan Hayward (I Want to Live)	Vicente Minnelli (Gigi)
1959	Ben-Hur	Charlton Heston (Ben-Hur)	Simone Signoret (Room at the Top)	William Wyler (Ben-Hur)
1960	The Apartment	Burt Lancaster (Elmer Gantry)	Elizabeth Taylor (Butterfield 8)	Billy Wilder (The Apartment)

Cartoons, or *animated* films, began to use both sound and color. Cartoons are made by showing a series of drawings one after another so that the drawn pictures seem to move. Walt Disney, a famous American cartoonist, began by making short, silent black-and-white cartoons. His make-believe stars, Mickey Mouse and Donald Duck, became as popular as real actors. Disney made the first full-length color cartoon, *Snow White and the Seven Dwarfs*, in 1937.

Documentaries

Beginning in the 1920s, some moviemakers became interested in using movies to record events in real life. These were called *documentaries*. An American named Robert Flaherty made the first important documentary, *Nanook of the North*, in 1922. It showed the hardships of Eskimo life and the beauty of the Arctic. John Grierson made the first British documentary, *Drifters*, in 1929. It was about a fishing fleet at sea. Documentaries became a device for spreading information during World War II.

◀ **A table showing the main Academy Award winners since the "Oscars" began.**

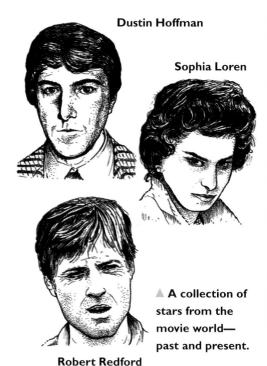

Dustin Hoffman

Sophia Loren

▲ A collection of stars from the movie world— past and present.

Robert Redford

Challenge to American Motion Picture Making

Just as radio took away early silent movie customers, television also had its effect on motion picture audiences. Some people began to stay home and watch movies on television. Others began to prefer the simpler, more realistic movies being made by European filmmakers. Hollywood moviemakers tried to fight back by using sensational techniques in movies. They developed Cinemascope and Cinerama with a larger screen and stereophonic sound, which made the audience feel as if the movie was going on all around them. *The Robe*, a Biblical story, was shown in 1953. *Around the World in 80 Days, South Pacific*, and *The Sound of Music* followed. Dazzling new color techniques and 3-D (3-dimensional) movies were also perfected. The 3-D movies made it seem as if images could jump right out of the screen into the audience. But viewers had to wear special glasses to watch the movies, and 3-D never really caught on.

2001: A Space Odyssey was an experimental Cinerama (wraparound screen) movie. Viewers felt

Year	Best Picture	Best Actor	Best Actress	Best Director
1961	West Side Story	Maximilian Schell (Judgment at Nurembourg)	Sophia Loren (Two Women)	Robert Wise & Jerome Robbins (West Side Story)
1962	Lawrence of Arabia	Gregory Peck (To Kill a Mockingbird)	Anne Bancroft (The Miracle Worker)	David Lean (Lawrence of Arabia)
1963	Tom Jones	Sidney Poitier (Lilies of the Field)	Patricia Neal (Hud)	Tony Richardson (Tom Jones)
1964	My Fair Lady	Rex Harrison (My Fair Lady)	Julie Andrews (Mary Poppins)	George Cukor (My Fair Lady)
1965	The Sound of Music	Lee Marvin (Cat Ballou)	Julie Christie (Darling)	Robert Wise (The Sound of Music)
1966	A Man for All Seasons	Paul Schofield (A Man For All Seasons)	Elizabeth Taylor (Who's Afraid of Virginia Woolf?)	Fred Zinneman (A Man for All Seasons)
1967	In the Heat of the Night	Rod Steiger (In the Heat of the Night)	Katharine Hepburn (Guess Who's Coming to Dinner?)	Mike Nichols (The Graduate)
1968	Oliver	Cliff Robertson (Charly)	Katharine Hepburn (The Lion in Winter), Barbara Streisand (Funny Girl)	Sir Carol Reed (Funny Girl)
1969	Midnight Cowboy	John Wayne (True Grit)	Maggie Smith (The Prime of Miss Jean Brodie)	John Schlesinger (Midnight Cowboy)
1970	Patton	George C. Scott (Patton)	Glenda Jackson (Women in Love)	Franklin J. Schaffner (Patton)
1971	The French Connection	Gene Hackman (The French Connection)	Jane Fonda (Klute)	William Friedkin (The French Connection)
1972	The Godfather	Marlon Brando (The Godfather)	Liza Minnelli (Cabaret)	Robert Fosse (Cabaret)
1973	The Sting	Jack Lemmon (Save the Tiger)	Glenda Jackson (A Touch of Class)	George Roy Hill (The Sting)
1974	The Godfather, Part II	Art Carney (Harry and Tonto)	Ellen Burstyn (Alice Doesn't Live Here Anymore)	Francis Ford Coppola (The Godfather, Part II)
1975	One Flew Over the Cuckoo's Nest	Jack Nicholson (One Flew Over the Cuckoo's Nest)	Louise Fletcher (One Flew Over the Cuckoo's Nest)	Milos Forman (One Flew Over the Cuckoo's Nest)
1976	Rocky	Peter Finch (Network)	Fay Dunaway (Network)	John G. Avildsen (Rocky)
1977	Annie Hall	Richard Dreyfus (The Goodbye Girl)	Diane Keaton (Annie Hall)	Woody Allen (Annie Hall)
1978	The Deerhunter	John Voight (Coming Home)	Jane Fonda (Coming Home)	Michael Cimino (The Deerhunter)
1979	Kramer vs. Kramer	Dustin Hoffman (Kramer vs. Kramer)	Sally Field (Norma Rae)	Robert Benton (Kramer vs. Kramer)
1980	Ordinary People	Robert de Niro (Raging Bull)	Sissy Spacek (Coal Miner's Daughter)	Robert Redford (Ordinary People)
1981	Chariots of Fire	Henry Fonda (On Golden Pond)	Katharine Hepburn (On Golden Pond)	Warren Beatty (Reds)
1982	Gandhi	Ben Kingsley (Gandhi)	Meryl Streep (Sophie's Choice)	Sir Richard Attenborough (Gandhi)
1983	Terms of Endearment	Robert Duvall (Tender Mercies)	Shirley MacLaine (Terms of Endearment)	James L. Brooks (Terms of Endearment)
1984	Amadeus	F. Murray Abraham (Amadeus)	Sally Field (Places in the Heart)	Milos Forman (Amadeus)
1985	Out of Africa	William Hurt (Kiss of the Spider Woman)	Geraldine Page (The Trip to Bountiful)	Sydney Pollack (Out of Africa)
1986	Platoon	Paul Newman (The Color of Money)	Marlee Martin (Children of a Lesser God)	Oliver Stone (Platoon)
1987	The Last Emperor	Michael Douglas (Wall Street)	Cher (Moonstruck)	Bernardo Bertolucci (The Last Emperor)
1988	Rain Man	Dustin Hoffman (Rain Man)	Jodie Foster (The Accused)	Barry Levinson (Rain Man)
1989	Driving Miss Daisy	Daniel Day-Lewis (My Left Foot)	Jessica Tandy (Driving Miss Daisy)	Oliver Stone (Born on the Fourth of July)
1990	Dances With Wolves	Jeremy Irons (Reversal of Fortune)	Kathy Bates (Misery)	Kevin Costner (Dances With Wolves)
1991	The Silence of the Lambs	Anthony Hopkins (The Silence of the Lambs)	Jodie Foster (The Silence of the Lambs)	Jonathan Demme (The Silence of the Lambs)
1992	Unforgiven	Al Pacino (Scent of a Woman)	Emma Thompson (Howard's End)	Clint Eastwood (Unforgiven)
1993	Schindler's List	Tom Hanks (Philadelphia)	Holly Hunter (The Piano)	Steven Spielberg (Schindler's List)

▲ A still from the popular movie *Honey, I Blew Up the Kids*. The film relies on a mix of comedy and clever special effects. It is also a sequel to the successful *Honey, I Shrunk the Kids*.

▲ The Academy Award is a gold-plated bronze statue 10 inches (25 cm) high and 7 pounds (3.2 kg) in weight.

they were on a journey through space. Experimental techniques with light were used in this picture. The big Hollywood companies began to sell their movies to television and began to make special films just for television. Some of the Hollywood producers went out of business. Others began to imitate the realism in European films and make less expensive motion pictures.

Movies Today and Tomorrow

Today, motion pictures face a new challenge from home video cassette recorders (VCRs). For a small cost, people can now watch feature films in the comfort of their own homes, and fewer go to movie theaters regularly. Modern movies depend more on good stories and filming techniques than on glamorous stars and elaborate sets. Sometimes they are created for more than just amusement. Motion pictures help teach subjects in schools and colleges. The armed forces use educational films to train soldiers, too. Business executives use movies to train employees and to tell their customers about

their products. Many high schools and colleges offer courses in filmmaking. Even elementary school classes make films now.

Movies are not even 100 years old. But the British art historian Kenneth Clark predicted that people living 100 years from now will look back on filmmaking as the greatest art form of our century.

The Academy Awards

The Academy of Motion Picture Arts and Sciences was founded in 1927 by Louis B. Mayer and other leaders of the Hollywood film world. The academy is still going strong today and is made up of several thousand people in every area of moviemaking. Its main purpose is to help improve the art and science of filmmaking. The academy also honors outstanding achievements with its Academy Awards. The academy members vote on who should win.

Once each year in Hollywood, California, small gold statues are awarded for the best performances by actors and actresses in leading and supporting roles and for best direction, music, costume design, photography, writing, sound recording, and other areas of production. An award is also given for the best movie of the year. Each award is a statue of a man, nicknamed "Oscar."

The first movie to win an Oscar was *Wings* in 1928. The first film to capture all five major awards (Best Picture, Best Actor, Best Actress, Best Director, and Best Screenplay) was *It Happened One Night*, starring Claudette Colbert and Clark Gable, in 1934. Today, the Oscar ceremony is a much publicized event. Winning can mean box office success as well as artistic acclaim.

▶▶▶▶ **FIND OUT MORE** ◀◀◀◀

Actors and Acting; Camera; Cartooning; Disney, Walt; Drama; Makeup; Musical Comedy; Photography; Television; Theater

⚙ MOTOR

A motor can be defined as a device that changes any form of energy into mechanical energy or motion. An engine is a kind of motor that consumes fuel to convert energy into mechanical power, as in an automobile or truck. An *electric motor* is an arrangement of magnets and wire coils that changes a special kind of energy—electric current—into mechanical power or motion. Electric motors are used every day in all kinds of electrical equipment found in most homes. Refrigerators, vacuum cleaners, sewing machines, record players, irons, washing machines, and fans are run by electric motors.

The action of magnetism is the principle on which an electric motor is based. The relationship between electricity and magnetism was discovered in 1819, when Hans Christian Oersted found that a wire carrying an electric current has a magnetic field around it. In other words, he discovered that electricity and magnetism are related. Shortly after this, other scientists discovered that a piece of iron becomes a magnet when it is put inside a coil of wire carrying electric current. They also found that the coil and iron together, called an *electromagnet,* had even greater magnetism. The British scientist Michael Faraday first had the idea of putting this electromagnetism to work in the form of a motor.

Even today, the principle on which an electric motor operates is similar to Faraday's idea. Mechanical power or motion is produced because of the attraction of *unlike* magnetic fields for each other and the repulsion of *like* magnetic fields from each other. In the simplest motor, a loop or coil of wire is attached to a metal stick, or *shaft.* The shaft is then suspended between the two poles of a permanent magnet.

When electric current is sent

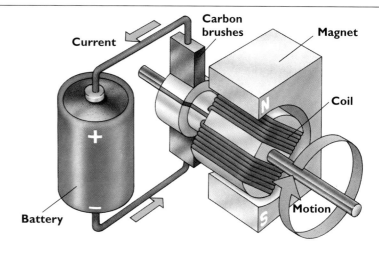

through the wire (perhaps from a battery), the unlike magnetic fields on the permanent magnet and electromagnet pull toward each other, and the like magnetic fields push away from each other. This causes the shaft and the wire to move in the same direction—forward, up, and down—depending on the location of the poles of the permanent magnet. When the electric current going through the wire is reversed, or sent in the opposite direction, the magnetic fields in the electromagnet are also reversed. This causes the shaft to move again—in the opposite direction. A steady movement of the motor is produced by a pair of metal strips, or *brushes*, connected to the battery or other power source. The brushes alternately touch the wire as it rotates on the shaft and provide a regular feeding of electric current. The regular reversal of the direction of the current keeps the shaft and the electromagnet moving. This movement is the power that is generated by a motor to operate a machine.

The more electric current given to a motor, the more power the motor generates. An electric fan motor, for example, produces more mechanical power than the motor in an electric clock does. Therefore, a fan motor uses more current.

▶▶▶▶ **FIND OUT MORE** ◀◀◀◀
Electric Appliance; Electricity; Electromagnet; Engine; Faraday, Michael; Magnet

▲ **An electric motor. A current turns the coil into an electromagnet, which the magnet poles force to spin.**

▲ **Many household appliances are run by electric motors; something most of us take for granted until a power blackout occurs.**

▼ The 1885 Daimler had no brakes, no lights, no suspension, and no gears. But it served as a model for early motorcycles.

▲ The 1911 American Indian had a sophisticated engine for its time. It proved a winning bike at the early testing races.

MOTORBOAT

SEE BOATS AND BOATING

MOTORCYCLE

When gasoline and steam engines were first developed, people began trying to find a practical way of attaching a motor to a bicycle. The result, later called a motorcycle, would be faster than a bicycle and less tiring to operate. In 1885, Gottlieb Daimler, a German inventor, attached a gasoline engine to a bicycle. His invention was the model for early motorcycles.

Today, however, motorcycles do not look nearly so much like bicycles. They are much wider and heavier than bikes. A motorcycle has an engine, which is mounted between the two wheels, with a gas tank above it. The driver sits astride the cycle on a padded *saddle,* or seat. Front and rear *springs*

▲ The British rider Joey Dunlop, who won the Isle of Man TT races in 1985 and again in 1988.

make the ride fairly comfortable for the motorcyclist.

The driver starts the motorcycle with the *starter button* on the handle bars or the *starter crank pedal* below the seat (operated with the foot). He or she shifts gears by pressing the *clutch hand lever* on the left handle-bar and the *gear shift* (below the engine) with the left foot. The driver stops the motorcycle by using the *front brake hand lever* on the right handlebar and the *rear brake foot pedal* beside the motorcycle engine.

There are various kinds of motor-cycles. A *touring bike* weighs several hundred pounds, can carry heavy loads, and can go at a high speed. It is often used for cross-country travel. A *trail bike* is not as heavy and fast as a

▶ A trail bike is a motorcycle made specially for riding over rough ground. It has shock absorbers to cushion bumps and knobbly patterned tires to grip sand and mud.

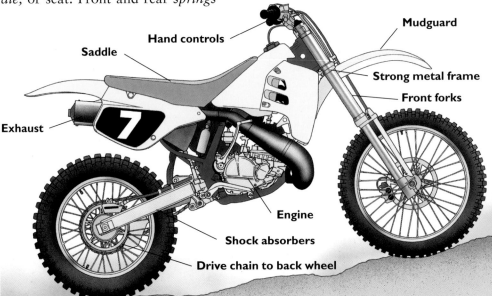

Hand controls

Saddle

Mudguard

Strong metal frame

Front forks

Exhaust

Engine

Shock absorbers

Drive chain to back wheel

touring bike. It is used on rugged country trails and for climbing steep hills. A *motor scooter* is smaller than an ordinary motorcycle, and the driver's feet rest on a floorboard, not astride a saddle as in a motorcycle. There are also *minicycles* (compact, sturdy motorcycles), *minibikes* (light-weight bikes with motorcycle-type engines), and *mopeds* (motorized bicycles).

Many cyclists compete in annual events (such as a motorcross rally) held in the United States, Canada, and other countries. Most of the U.S. events are governed by the American Motorcycle Association (AMA).

Motorcycles are a popular form of transportation. They are more fuel-efficient and cheaper to buy and operate than cars, and they are faster than bicycles. They can be dangerous, however, and it is important for cyclists to wear proper safety equipment and observe the rules of safe biking at all times. The police often use motorcycles, especially three-wheeled ones, because the motorcycle's small size enables officers to move easily through traffic.

▶▶▶ **FIND OUT MORE** ◀◀◀
Bicycle; Engine; Gear; Motor

MOUND BUILDERS

SEE IOWA

MOUNTAIN

All over the Earth, the giant rigid plates that form the Earth's crust are slowly moving. When they collide, the rocks in between are squeezed until they buckle, forming mountains. These are called *fold* mountains, and they form some of the highest and most extensive mountain ranges in the world. The Appalachian Mountains are an example of very old fold mountains.

The lowland between mountains is called a *valley*, through which streams and rivers flow.

Block mountains are formed when huge masses of rock move up or down along cracks, or *faults*, in the Earth's surface. Steep cliffs result from this type of Earth movement. The Sierra Nevada Mountains in California are an example of block mountains. Earthquakes are also caused by these Earth shifts.

Another way a mountain can be born is through *volcanic action*. Molten rock deep in the Earth forces its way up to the surface. On February 20, 1943, an extraordinary eruption occurred in a cornfield in west central Mexico. A new volcano, Parícutin, pushed up through the Earth's crust. Showers of hot rocks and lava burst through an opening in the earth. The cinder cone formed by the ashes was 100 feet (30 m) high by the second day. It was 450 feet (137 m) high two weeks later. When it stopped erupting in 1952, the cone of Parícutin was about 2,000 feet (610 m) high. Volcanic action can also push the earth up into *dome* mountains. These high, rounded mountains are like blisters full of hot liquid when they are first formed. But

▲ Mount Fuji, Japan's highest mountain, is a volcano that was last active in 1707. It reaches a height of 12,355 feet (3,766 meters) above sea level, and often the top is hidden by clouds. The Japanese believe it to be sacred. Thousands of pilgrims climb it each year.

Strange as it seems, the rock strata formed in the world's highest mountain chain, the Himalayas, began at the bottom of a great sea. Over millions of years, the rock has been lifted and folded into mountains such as Everest.

Where is the highest known mountain? Strangely enough, it is not Mount Everest and it is not on Earth. It is Olympus Mons (Mount Olympus) on Mars, and is 95,000 feet (29,000 m) high—over three times as high as Mount Everest.

▶ The Himalayas, the world's highest fold mountains, were pushed up where the Indian subcontinent met the continent of Asia.

The higher you go up a mountain, the colder it gets. The temperature drops by 3°F for every 1,000 feet (5°C for every 300 m) you go up.

▼ Different kinds of fold mountains. A *nappe* is a fold pushed forward over the rocks. A fold may be tilted over to form a *recumbent* fold. Below, opposite page, shows how block mountains are thrown up. These are called *horsts*; the steep slopes bordering them are *fault scarps*.

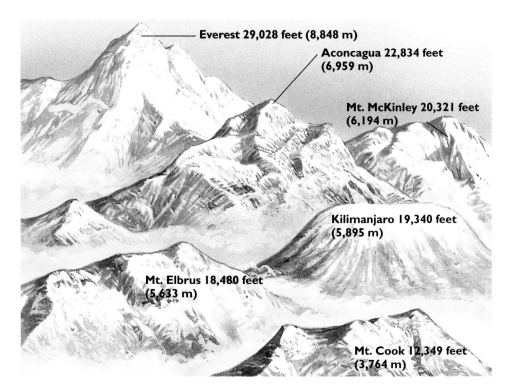

Everest 29,028 feet (8,848 m)

Aconcagua 22,834 feet (6,959 m)

Mt. McKinley 20,321 feet (6,194 m)

Kilimanjaro 19,340 feet (5,895 m)

Mt. Elbrus 18,480 feet (5,633 m)

Mt. Cook 12,349 feet (3,764 m)

the liquid later cools and forms solid rock. Elk Mountain in Wyoming is a dome mountain.

No sooner is a mountain formed then *erosion* sets in. Wind, rain, frost, and snow slowly wear away the rock and produce an endless variety of mountain shapes.

The highest mountain on land is Mount Everest: 29,028 feet (8,848 m) high. But the Earth's greatest mountains lie beneath the sea. They are higher and more rugged than those on land because they are not worn down by erosion. The tips of some undersea mountains form islands in the middle of the ocean. Mauna Loa,

the famous volcano on the island of Hawaii, is the tip of an undersea mountain.

Plants that only grow high up on mountains are called *alpine* plants. Trees will usually not survive any higher than about 11,000 feet (3,350 m). The point where alpine shrubs, mosses, and bare rock replace trees is called the *timberline*. A number of animals can live in the wind, cold, poor vegetation, and thin air of the mountains. Some of the best-known mountain animals in North America are the bighorn sheep, Rocky Mountain goat, marmot, snowshoe rabbit, and mountain lion. People, too, can

Nappe   Recumbent fold   Anticline   Syncline   Anticlinorium

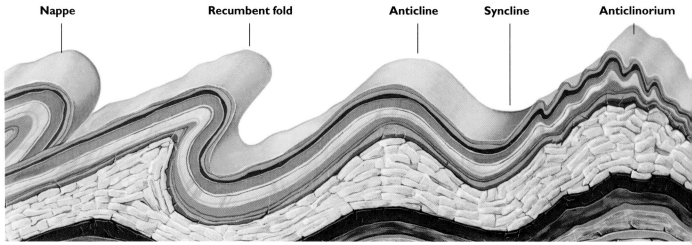

INTERESTING MOUNTAINS IN THE SEVEN CONTINENTS OF THE WORLD				
NAME	HEIGHT (IN FEET)	HEIGHT (IN METERS)	LOCATION	POINT OF INTEREST
AFRICA Kilimanjaro— (has 2 peaks)				Highest mountain in Africa
Kibo	19,340	5,895	Tanzania	
Mawenzi	17,564	5,354	Tanzania	
ANTARCTICA Vinson Massif	16,860	5,139	Chilean sector	Highest mountain in Antarctica
ASIA Everest	29,028	8,848	Nepal-Tibet border	Highest mountain in Asia and the world
Fuji	12,389	3,776	Japan	Sacred mountain to many Japanese
Nebo	2,625	800	Jordan	Peak from which Moses looked out at the Promised Land
AUSTRALIA Kosciusko	7,316	2,230	New South Wales	Highest mountain in Australia
EUROPE Elbrus	18,480	5,633	Russia	Highest mountain in Europe
Matterhorn	14,780	4,505	Switzerland-Italy border	Skilled mountain climbers scale its peak
Mount Etna	10,902	3,323	Italy	Active volcano in Europe
Vesuvius	4,200	1,280	Italy	Active volcano in Europe
NORTH AMERICA McKinley	20,321	6,194	Alaska	Highest mountain in North America
Pikes Peak	14,110	4,301	Colorado	First peak of the Rockies that can be seen by people coming from the east
Lassen Peak	10,446	3,190	California	Active volcano in the contiguous U.S.
St. Helens	9,677	2,950	Washington	Active volcano in the contiguous U.S.
SOUTH AMERICA Aconcagua	22,834	6,959	Argentina	Highest mountain in South America
Cotopaxi	19,347	5,897	Ecuador	Highest active volcano in the world

live at high altitudes. Mountain climbers from the lowlands often bring an oxygen supply with them. But the Indians of the Andes and the mountain people of the Himalayas have adapted to the thin air.

Mountains have long played an important part throughout history in deciding boundaries between countries. The Pyrenees separate France from Spain. The Himalayas provide a high barrier between India and China. Mountains have checked conquering armies and often forced them to retreat. A gap through a mountain range can often prove important in history. The Cumberland Gap in the Appalachian Mountains provided a passageway to the West for thousands of American pioneers.

▶▶▶▶ **FIND OUT MORE** ◀◀◀◀

Alps Mountains; Andes Mountains; Appalachian Mountains; Atmosphere; Canyon; Caucasus Mountains; Earthquake; Erosion; Geology; Himalaya Mountains; Mountain Climbing; Rocky Mountains; Ural Mountains; Volcano

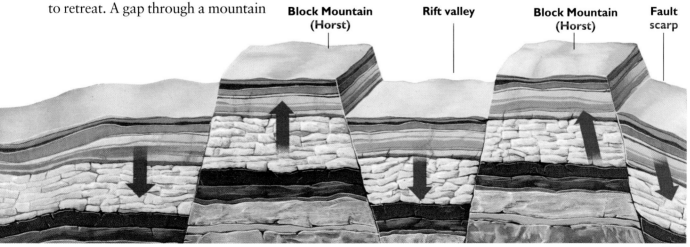

Block Mountain (Horst)   Rift valley   Block Mountain (Horst)   Fault scarp

▲ Ice axes are being used for cutting out footholds to allow the climbers a firmer grip on the slippery slope.

▲ Mountaineers Sir Edmund Hillary and Sherpa Tenzing Norgay. They were the first to reach the top of Mount Everest, on May 29, 1953.

MOUNTAIN CLIMBING

Mountain climbing is a sport in which men and women climb the slopes of hills and mountains on foot. *Mountaineers* (climbers) must be in excellent physical condition and must be experienced in climbing techniques in order to survive.

In Great Britain, the craggy hills of Wales and Scotland are popular with mountaineers. The high peaks of the Alps in Europe attract climbers from many countries. The Andes Mountains in South America and the Himalayas in Asia also offer challenges to mountain climbers. The Rockies in the United States have many peaks that attract mountaineering fans.

Mountain climbing clubs have been established for people interested in the sport. The oldest, England's Alpine Club, was established in 1858. Clubs in this country include the American Alpine Club, the Sierra Club, and the Appalachian Mountain Club. These and similar organizations train climbers and interested beginners in the best and safest methods of climbing.

Many special kinds of equipment are used in mountain climbing. Climbers wear heavy boots with cleated soles to prevent slipping on steep inclines. To climb on ice, mountaineers attach *crampons,* frames with special steel spikes, to their boots. When climbers travel over steep rocks and icy slopes, they are often tied to each other with long ropes. Then one person at a time moves forward. If someone slips, the others, who are tied to that person, can prevent him or her from falling too far. Iron spikes called *pitons* may be driven into the rock to provide footholds or places to attach ropes. Climbers carry ice axes to cut footholds in ice. They are also used as walking sticks. Climbers wear dark glasses to protect their eyes from the blinding snow and insulated clothing to keep themselves warm. Climbers wear backpacks containing first aid, cooking equipment, and food. If the climb is to take more than one day, they must carry tents and sleeping bags in their backpacks. If the peak is very high, where the air has little oxygen, climbers bring tanks of oxygen with them.

Mountain climbing first became popular in Europe in the 1800s. Expeditions of mountaineers began climbing the highest and most difficult peaks in the world during the 1900s. In 1953, Sir Edmund Hillary and Tenzing Norgay reached the summit of Mount Everest, the world's highest mountain. Some of the world's highest peaks still remain to be conquered.

▶▶▶▶ **FIND OUT MORE** ◀◀◀◀
Hillary, Sir Edmund; Himalaya Mountains; Mountain

MOUNT VERNON

SEE WASHINGTON, GEORGE

MOUSE

SEE RATS AND MICE

MOVIE

SEE MOTION PICTURE

MOZAMBIQUE

Mozambique, formerly called Portuguese East Africa, is bounded by Tanzania on the north, Malawi and Zambia on the northwest, Zimbabwe on the west, and South Africa on the southwest. The east coast stretches along the Indian Ocean for 1,736 miles (2,794 km).

Mozambique's ports are important for importing goods to the African interior and for exporting goods to the rest of the world. Maputo, the capital and largest city, is an important seaport. Beira is the other leading seaport.

There are lowlands along the coast of Mozambique and high, grassy open plains, called *savannas*, in the interior. Mozambique is a hot, tropical country with seasonal rainy and dry periods. Farming is the most important industry. Sugarcane, corn, cotton, coconuts, tea, and other crops are grown, usually on large plantations. It is the world's leading producer of cashew nuts. Mozambique has rich mineral deposits, which have been only partially mined.

In 1498, Vasco da Gama, a Portuguese navigator, was the first European to explore the coastal area of Mozambique. The Portuguese founded settlements along the coast during the 1500s, and Mozambique was a colony of Portugal for 470 years. Slavery was commonplace in Mozambique from the late 1500s until the present century. Slaves captured in the interior were often shipped out and sold in other parts of the world, especially Brazil, until the middle 1800s. Slavery was completely abolished in Mozambique after 1928.

Most of the people of Mozambique are black Africans who speak one of several Bantu languages. The largest group, making up 40 percent of the population, are the Makua-Lomwe. There are also some Portuguese, Arabs, and Asians.

From 1964 until 1974, the Front for the Liberation of Mozambique (Frelimo) waged a guerrilla war against Portuguese colonial rule. In 1975, Mozambique became an independent nation. Its government was led by President Samora Machel until he died in a plane crash in 1986. Machel was succeeded as president by Joaquim Chissano. Since independence, Mozambique has had a Socialist government allied to the former U.S.S.R. It has suffered droughts and a civil war, with government troops fighting a right-wing guerrilla force, the Mozambique National Resistance.

MOZAMBIQUE

Capital city
Maputo
(1,072,000 people)

Area
309,496 square miles
(801,590 sq. km)

Population
14,800,000 people

Government
People's republic

Natural resources
Coal, iron, ore, diamonds, gold, natural gas, titanium

Export products
Shrimps, cashew nuts, sugar, copra, cotton, citrus fruit

Unit of money
Metical

Official language
Portuguese

Lake Nyasa
Mocimboa da Praia
Rovuma R.
Lugenda R.
Lichinga
Pemba
Lurio R.
Nacala
Nampula
Mocambique
L. Cabora Bassa
R. Chiluva
Tete
Zambezi R.
Quelimane
Chimoio
Mt. Binga 7,992 ft. 2,436 m.
Beira
Buzi R.
Save R.
Mozambique Channel
Changane R.
Vilanculos
Limpopo R.
Inhambane
Xai-Xai
INDIAN OCEAN
Maputo

N
W — E
S

0   200   400 Miles
0   200   400   600 Kilometers
© 1994 GeoSystems, an R.R. Donnelley & Sons Company

▶ ▶ ▶ ▶ **FIND OUT MORE** ◀ ◀ ◀ ◀
Africa; Portugal; Slavery

▲ Wolfgang Amadeus Mozart. He only lived for 35 years, but became one of the world's finest composers.

▼ When Beethoven first went to Vienna in 1787, he played in front of Mozart, who was very impressed.

MOZART, WOLFGANG AMADEUS (1756–1791)

The great eighteenth-century composer Wolfgang Amadeus Mozart began to write music when he was 5 years old. He was giving public concerts of his own music at the age of 6. Although Mozart had a short and tragic life, his works have remained among the world's greatest classical musical compositions.

Mozart was born in Salzburg, Austria. His father, Leopold Mozart, was a composer and violinist. He gave Wolfgang and his elder sister, Maria Anna, musical training and took them on concert tours throughout Europe. The two children gave many public performances on the *harpsichord* (an early type of piano) and even played for kings and queens. Everyone was amazed at Wolfgang's talents. He never went to school, but he learned about different musical styles from other musicians.

At the age of 14, Mozart became concertmaster at the court of the archbishop of Salzburg. The young musician was poorly paid there, and he was constantly trying to find a better job. He finally left the archbishop in 1781 and went to live in Vienna. He married and tried to support his family by giving music

lessons and working day and night at his compositions, but he became very poor. In 1787, Mozart was appointed court composer to the Austrian emperor.

A mysterious stranger asked Mozart to compose a *requiem mass* (music for a funeral service) in 1791. Mozart was very ill at the time and he died before his *Requiem* was finished. A pupil later completed it.

Mozart wrote more than 600 musical compositions. His music has a lively, vigorous spirit and beautiful melodies that still sound fresh. He wrote several lovely operas, such as *The Magic Flute* and *Don Giovanni*, and many symphonies.

▶▶▶▶ **FIND OUT MORE** ◀◀◀◀
Composer

MUHAMMAD (about A.D. 570–632)

Muhammad was the founder of Islam, one of the world's great religions. He was born in the Arabian city of Mecca, a busy trading and religious center. Muhammad's family belonged to the ruling tribe of Quraish in Mecca. His parents died when Muhammad was a baby, and he was raised by his uncle.

Muhammad became a camel driver and later a merchant and traveled a few times with trading caravans. He was deeply religious and spent many hours in prayer. The Arab tribes at the time worshiped many gods. But Muhammad believed in only one true God. When he was 40 years old, he began to have visions. He believed that the angel Gabriel appeared and told him to teach the words of God. His wife, Khadija, believed in his visions, and soon he had other followers, who called him the prophet of God. The words that he heard in his visions were written down and later collected in the *Koran*.

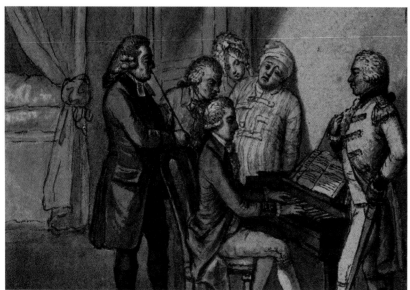

Muhammad angered the merchants of Mecca by criticizing their greedy lives. He was persecuted in Mecca and was forced to flee to Medina, a nearby city, in A.D. 622. This flight is called the *Hegira,* and the Muslim calendar dates from it. He was invited to Medina to make peace between warring tribes, and he even became governor. In A.D. 630, Muhammad returned to Mecca and captured the city. Most of the people were converted to Islam.

Muhammad died two years later, but the faith of Islam spread rapidly. Its followers, Muslims or Moslems, number about 550 million. Islam forbids images, or likenesses, so no pictures or statues of Muhammad were ever made. The *Sunna,* or traditions, is a record of the sayings and deeds of Muhammad collected after his death by Muslim leaders.

▶▶▶▶ **FIND OUT MORE** ◀◀◀◀
Islam; Koran; Mosque

MULE

SEE DONKEY

MULRONEY, BRIAN (1939–)

Martin Brian Mulroney, Canada's prime minister from 1984 to 1993, was born on March 20, 1939, in the town of Bale Comeau in Quebec province. He grew up speaking both English and fluent French. He studied at Saint Francis Xavier University in Nova Scotia and at Laval University in Quebec City, graduating with a law degree in 1962. He joined the Progressive-Conservative Party and tried unsuccessfully to win the party leadership in 1976.

In 1983, Mulroney became party leader. Although he was not well known, he led his party to a landslide victory in the 1984 general election. As prime minister, he sought agreements with the U.S. government on defense. In 1988, Mulroney was reelected with a decisive majority. He immediately introduced a controversial free-trade agreement with the United States. In 1991, he tried to recapture his dwindling popularity with a major cabinet reshuffle. In June 1993, he was succeeded by Kim Campbell from British Columbia, Canada's first female prime minister, who served until Jean Chretien, a Liberal, was elected in October 1993.

▶▶▶▶ **FIND OUT MORE** ◀◀◀◀
Canada; Political Party

MULTIPLE BIRTH

SEE REPRODUCTION

MULTIPLICATION

SEE ARITHMETIC, MATHEMATICS

MUMPS

SEE CHILDHOOD DISEASES

MURDER

Murder is the killing of a human being on purpose and without legal justification (self-defense). It is considered the most serious crime.

There are different kinds of murder recognized by law in the United

◀ **Muhammad, the founder of the Islamic religion. Islam tradition dictates that idols are not permitted. For this reason, artists are forbidden to draw or paint his face.**

▲ **Martin Brian Mulroney, usually known simply as Brian Mulroney, was prime minister of Canada from 1984 to 1993.**

There are situations where a killing is considered murder, even if there was no initial intent to kill. For example, if a victim is killed during a robbery, the law deems that the robbers, without due regard for human life and safety, were involved in a serious crime and the death is regarded as murder.

▼ The Darling River and the Murray River in Australia meet at Wentworth to become the Murray-Darling, which empties into the Indian Ocean. Flowing slowly, it is easily navigable and was once used for commercial transportation of goods. Here, people on a houseboat enjoy the spectacular scenery.

States. *Justifiable homicide* is a killing that has legal justification, such as murder in self-defense. *Excusable homicide* is an accidental killing, such as a person walking in front of a carefully driven car and being killed. If a person is killed because of a car driver's *negligence* (failure to act wisely), it is called *involuntary manslaughter. Voluntary manslaughter* is killing a person in anger, after being *provoked* (aroused) by the victim.

A murderer may be sent to a state or federal prison or *penitentiary* for a long period (sometimes for life) or may be put to death. The death penalty, however, has been abolished in many U.S. states and in many countries.

▶▶▶▶ **FIND OUT MORE** ◀◀◀◀
Crime; Trial

 MURRAY-DARLING RIVERS

The Great Dividing Range of mountains extends along the eastern coast of Australia. Water from rain and melting snow on the western slopes of the mountains runs down into several rivers. The longest of these is the Darling River, which flows southwest for about 1,700 miles (2,740 km). At Wentworth, Australia, the Darling joins the Murray River, which has already flowed northwest for 1,600 miles (2,575 km) from the Australian Alps (part of the Great Dividing Range). The Murray-Darling, sometimes just called the Murray River, then travels southward to empty into the Indian Ocean, near Adelaide. The Murray River, 2,310 miles (3,715 km) long from the mountains to the ocean, is Australia's longest river. It and its tributaries drain an area larger than that of Texas, Oklahoma, and Louisiana combined. (See the map with the article on AUSTRALIA.)

Both the Darling and the Murray rivers flow very slowly. The Darling River often dries up completely in years when there is very little rain. The Murray is the only river in Australia that can be navigated for long distances. Side-wheeled steamboats once traveled up and down the river carrying wool, grain, and other commercial products. Today, these goods are transported by trains and trucks.

Engineers have devised ways to add more water to the Murray River. Reservoirs and dams were built high in the mountains of the Great Dividing Range to catch water that would normally have run off down the eastern slopes.

▶▶▶▶ **FIND OUT MORE** ◀◀◀◀
Australia; River

 **MUSCLE**

Bones and various organs of the body cannot move by themselves. They are moved by muscles. The human body contains more than 600 main muscles and thousands of very small ones.

Muscles move by *contracting.* Muscle cells seem able to bunch together to make the muscle shorter or more compact. Muscle contraction is caused by *myofibril* chains of protein inside the muscle cells. These

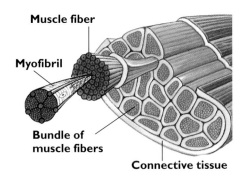

Muscle fiber

Myofibril

Bundle of muscle fibers

Connective tissue

▲ The interior of a muscle looks like a bundle of cables. These cables are muscle fibers, surrounded by connective tissue. Each fiber is in turn made up of strands of myofibrils, which contain two types of protein: myosin and actin.

protein chains seem to be able to slide over each other and make the muscle contract.

Muscles are divided into three types: skeletal, smooth, and cardiac. Most *skeletal muscles* are attached to bones by tough white cords called *tendons*. The muscles of the face have no tendons and are attached directly to the bone. Both ends of a muscle are attached to the bone.

Skeletal muscles vary in size, depending on the work they do. The muscles that move your eyeballs are smaller and weaker than the muscles that move your legs. Skeletal muscles are of two kinds. The *flexors* bend a joint or contract inward toward the body. When you bend your elbow or make a fist, you are using flexor muscles. The *extensors* straighten a joint or pull outward away from the body. When you straighten your arm or open your fist, you are using extensors.

Skeletal muscles contain nerves. The nerves send a *stimulus*, or signal, to the muscles to make them contract. The stimulus can be a signal from the brain to the nerves. When you want to grasp a pencil, your brain sends signals to the nerves that control your finger, hand, and arm muscles. These muscles then contract, moving your hand and arm to the proper position. The stimulus can also come from outside your body. When you touch something hot, the

▶ The skeleton performs the important job of protecting the soft parts of the body, such as the brain.

Skull (cranium)

Jawbone (mandible)

Neck vertebrae

Collar bone (clavicle)

Shoulder blade (scapula)

Rib cage

Back (lumbar) vertebrae

Main forearm bone (ulna)

Small forearm bone (radius)

Hipbone (pelvis)

Wrist bone (carpals)

Frontal muscle

Temporal muscle

Chewing muscle (masseter)

Neck muscles

Shoulder muscle (deltoid)

Chest muscles (pectorals)

Lower arm (brachiordialis)

Abdominal muscle (rectus abdominis)

▶ As well as giving the body a framework, the skeleton also works with the muscles to move the body. This is made very clear by looking at the shoulder, wrist, hip, and knee joints. There are approximately 206 bones in the human body, some of which are *fused*, joined, together.

Thigh bone (femur)

Kneecap (patella)

Small shin bone (fibula)

Main shin bone (tibia)

Thigh muscle (sartorius)

Calf muscle (gastrocnemius)

◀ Skeletal muscles, like the calf muscles, are attached to the bones and are consciously controlled.

nerves sense the heat and send a stimulus to your muscles that makes you jerk your hand away. This is called a *reflex* action. Skeletal muscles cannot contract if they are unable to receive a stimulus from the nerves. When nerves are damaged and unable to stimulate certain muscles, these muscles are *paralyzed*.

Most skeletal muscles are voluntary. Voluntary means that you may consciously use your brain to control the action of the muscle. Involuntary means that the muscle works without your help. The diaphragm below your chest controls your breathing.

Triceps contracts

Biceps contracts

Biceps relaxed

Triceps relaxed

▲ When you bend your arm, the muscles work in pairs. The biceps bend the arm, the triceps straighten it.

A cramp is the continuous contraction of a muscle. This painful complaint is often caused by a lack of oxygen in the muscle, usually after violent exercise. A cramp also may be caused by poor blood circulation or by swimming in cold water too soon after a meal.

It has been calculated that you use more than 200 different muscles when you walk.

▼ The frog is well known for its amazing leaping ability. Strong back leg muscles are needed to accelerate the body from a sitting start. The leg joints straighten like a series of levers from the hip to the knee and ankle.

Lower leg bones

Foot bones

Toe bones

Hip and thigh muscles

Muscles pull bones

Lower leg muscles

Hip and thigh muscles

It is an involuntary muscle because it can work without your thinking about it. When you take control of the diaphragm by thinking about breathing, it works as a voluntary muscle.

Smooth muscles are not attached to bones, but are contained in various body organs. Smooth muscles in the stomach and intestines slowly contract and relax to move food that is being digested. Muscles in the blood vessels control blood flow.

All smooth muscles are involuntary. You cannot control them. These muscles may also work without stimuli from nerves. Their contractions are controlled by hormones. When you are angry or afraid, for example, your adrenal glands produce hormones that contract muscles in certain arteries, especially those that feed major internal organs. This forces more blood to your brain and skeletal muscles to make you more alert and prepare you for fighting or running. *Cardiac muscle* is the muscle of the heart. It is an involuntary muscle and is the only type of muscle that can contract in a definite rhythm. Scientists do not know what causes the cardiac muscle to contract this way. They do know that the heart has a built-in pacemaker. A stimulus received from the nerves can speed up or slow down the beat, but cannot control the rhythm.

Besides nerve or hormone stimulus, all muscles need energy in order to work. Energy is supplied from the food you eat. Muscle cells contain *enzymes* that constantly break down digested food and turn it into energy. Muscle cells can store energy in the form of a substance called ATP (adenosine tri-phosphate). When energy is needed, the ATP is released.

If you use your muscles for a long time, waste material collects in the muscle tissue, and your muscles lose some of their ability to contract. This is called *muscle fatigue*. Your body feels tired and needs rest in order to remove the wastes.

Muscles get bigger if they are given a great deal of use. A ballet dancer's leg muscles or a weight lifter's arm and shoulder muscles are usually larger than most people's. Muscles become smaller if they are not used. Paralyzed muscles eventually shrink to a small size.

People whose muscles contract quickly and powerfully are said to have good muscle tone. Muscles can get out of tone by not having enough exercise. Muscle tone can be improved with more exercise. But too much exercise of a muscle that is not prepared for it can cause *muscle strain*. The muscle stretches or tears and soreness results.

▶▶▶▶ **FIND OUT MORE** ◀◀◀◀
Bone; Brain; Cell; Circulatory System; Digestion; Energy; Enzyme; Gland; Heart; Human Body; Nervous System

MUSES

The myths of ancient Greece tell of nine goddesses called the Muses. They were young maidens who watched over the arts and sciences. The Muses were the daughters of Zeus, king of the gods, and Mnemosyne, goddess of memory. They often entertained the other gods and goddesses on Mount Olympus with songs and stories.

Each Muse had a special art or science of her own, symbolized in Greek art by a particular sign. Clio, the Muse of history, carried a *scroll,* or rolled document. Thalia, who wore a comic mask, was the Muse of comedy and pastoral poetry. Calliope, the most honored of all the Muses, carried a writing tablet and *stylus* (writing tool). She was the Muse of *epic,* or heroic, poetry. Euterpe, who played the flute, was the Muse of lyric poetry. Melpomene, who wore a tragic mask and carried a sword, was the Muse of tragedy. Erato, the Muse of love poetry, and Terpsichore, the Muse of dancing and singing, both carried stringed instruments called *lyres.* Polyhymnia, the Muse of *hymns,* or sacred songs, wore a veil over her face. Urania, the Muse of astronomy, was pictured with a globe. The ancient Greeks prayed to the Muses for inspiration before beginning any artistic, literary, or scientific project.

▶▶▶▶ **FIND OUT MORE** ◀◀◀◀
Gods and Goddesses; Greece, Ancient; Mythology

MUSEUM

Have you ever wanted to see how prehistoric people or the colonial Americans lived? Did you ever wish you could go inside a submarine or see inside the tomb of an Egyptian pharaoh? You *can* see these things— at a museum.

Museums are places where great collections are kept. Perhaps you collect things, such as stamps, marbles, cards, coins, or model cars. Museums collect and take care of valuable art works, historical objects, and scientific objects.

The director of a museum has several *curators* working under him or her. Each curator is in charge of a separate type of collection. The director and curators must get new items for the museum's collection. They do this by buying or trading with other museums or with people who have

important objects to sell. Sometimes people who own valuable objects will give them to museums as a gift. Some museums that have a great deal of money send out scientific expeditions to find objects.

Museum workers keep records of every object in the collection. They number each object, write a detailed description of it, and photograph it. The description tells when, where, and how the object was found, the age and value of the object, and its importance.

Special museum workers called *conservators* clean each object and try to *restore* (repair) it by putting it back into good shape or working order. They also protect objects by treating and storing them safely.

Large museums do not show their whole collections at the same time. Only the most interesting or important objects are put on display. Most of the objects are stored away in *study collections* for scientists and historians to use. Study collections contain thousands of objects that are interesting only to experts in various subjects. The objects that are on display are grouped into *exhibits.* Dinosaur skeletons may be one kind of exhibit. Native American life may be another. A *permanent exhibit* stays at one museum. A *temporary exhibit* is a special collection that is

▲ **Terpsichore was one of the nine Muses, who represented the arts in ancient Greek mythology.**

▼ **The National Air and Space Museum in Washington, D.C., houses some of the earliest airplanes, including *Wright-Flyer I* (left) and the *Spirit of St. Louis* (right), as well as many of NASA's space rockets, capsules, and satellites.**

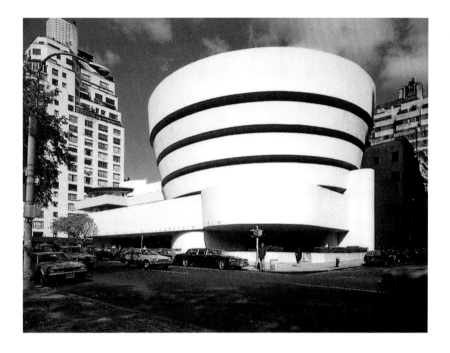

▲ The Guggenheim Museum, in New York City, houses an art collection. The impressive circular building was designed by the architect Frank Lloyd Wright.

▲ The bones of a mammoth on display at a museum of natural history. The bones have been reconstructed to form a skeleton so that visitors to the museum can get an idea of the size and appearance of this prehistoric creature.

sent around to various museums. Each museum displays it for a short time and then sends it on to another museum. This gives people in many places a chance to see the exhibit. Some museums have small *traveling exhibits* that are sent to schools or communities of people who cannot come to the museum.

Museums have guides who take groups of visitors around. Guides explain the exhibits and tell the history and importance of the objects. Museum displays always have labels that tell something about the objects, their history, how they were used, who used them, and other interesting facts. Large museums give courses in which you can learn about various historical or scientific subjects. Museums have speakers, usually experts in various fields, who give talks on interesting topics. Museums also show films and slides, and almost all museums have shops that sell pictures and small models of some of the objects on display. Most of the large museums publish magazines to which you can subscribe.

Kinds of Museums

HISTORY MUSEUMS. These museums collect objects that have important historical value. History museums may be very large, dealing with the history of the entire world. Smaller museums have collections that show the history of a particular place, such as a nation, city, or state. Some history museums are based on the life of a particular person, event, or group of people. The Lenin Museum in Moscow has collected a great number of objects connected with the life of Vladimir Lenin. The Gettysburg Museum in Gettysburg, Pennsylvania, tells the history of a U.S. Civil War battle. The DuSable Museum in Chicago, Illinois, tells of the history of black people.

The Smithsonian Institution in Washington, D.C., consists of many museums. Among the exhibits in its National Museum of History and Technology are the gowns worn by the wives of U.S. Presidents, the original Star-Spangled Banner that flew over Fort McHenry during the War of 1812, Samuel Morse's telegraph, automobiles, airplanes, trains, stamps, and coins.

ART MUSEUMS. Art museums contain collections of paintings, sculpture, drawings, handicrafts, and photography. Smaller art museums often concentrate on one kind of art. They collect the artwork of a certain area, of a certain time in history, or of a certain group of people.

NATURAL HISTORY MUSEUMS. Some museums collect plants and animals of the past and the present. They also exhibit rocks and fossil animals that show the history of the Earth. The Field Museum of Natural History in Chicago, Illinois, is a very large museum divided into four sections—*anthropology* (the study of human beings), *botany* (the study of plants), *geology* (the study of the Earth), and *zoology* (the study of animals). The exhibits include life-size panoramas of prehistoric people in their world; the most complete collection of meteorites in the world; and animals of different countries, shown in their natural environment. The National Museum of Anthropology in Mexico City has the largest collection based on people in the Mexican region.

SCIENCE MUSEUMS. These museums display industrial and scientific equipment and show how it is used.

At the Museum of Science and Industry in Chicago, Illinois, you can take a trip through a coal mine or see yourself on color television. You can climb aboard a full-sized submarine, stroll down a street set in the year 1910, watch chicks hatch, or see how nuclear energy works.

OTHER MUSEUMS. *Children's museums* display collections that will interest children. Many are "hands on" exhibits that can be tried out, such as a model telephone that lets you hear your own voice.

Folk museums are whole towns or groups of buildings that have been rebuilt or restored to their original condition. At a folk museum you can see how people of the past used to live. The town at Williamsburg, the colonial capital of Virginia, is a folk museum. You can walk through the old streets and into the buildings, houses, and shops. Guides dressed in colonial costume show you how Americans lived 250 years ago.

Libraries can be museums, too. The big libraries in large cities have collections of ancient books and writings.

If you travel to foreign countries, be sure to visit their museums. London has many museums of art and science. Paris has the Louvre, the world's greatest art museum. Leningrad has the Hermitage, and Madrid has the Prado.

▶ ▶ ▶ **FIND OUT MORE** ◀ ◀ ◀
Art Museums and Galleries;
Collecting; Zoo

MUSHROOM

Mushrooms have been connected with magic for hundreds of years. This may be due to the way they grow. On a warm spring or summer morning, especially after a rain, people have found mushrooms growing where there were none the day before. They seem to appear as if by magic. Actually, there is nothing magical about mushrooms. They are members of a group of plants called fungi. They cannot make their own food because they do not contain the green chlorophyll that other types of plants have. Mushrooms get their food by causing vegetable matter to decay. For this reason, mushrooms are often found growing on fallen logs as well as in the earth. Mushrooms are also called *toadstools*.

There are about 38,000 different kinds of mushrooms. They come in all colors except green and in various shapes and sizes. The part of a mushroom that grows underground or in decaying wood is called the *mycelium*. It holds the plant steady and takes in water and nourishment. Above ground is the mushroom *stipe*, or stem, topped by the cap. On the underside of the cap grow large numbers of *spores* on flat membranes called *gills*. Each spore acts like a seed. It drops to the ground and grows into a new mushroom

Oyster mushroom
(Pleurotus ostreatus)

▲ **The edible oyster mushroom grows in tiers on trees in late fall. It can be found in many supermarkets also.**

Field mushroom
(Agaricus campestris)

▲ **Found in meadows and pastures, this is a common mushroom that grows in abundance during the warm, early fall rains.**

Mushrooms may range in height from about ¾ inch (1.9 cm) to about 15 inches (38 cm), with diameters of less than ¼ inch (0.6 cm) to about 18 inches (46 cm).